Heart
to Heart

Incredible and heartwarming stories
from the woman who talks with animals

Heart
to Heart

PEA HORSLEY

HarperElement
An Imprint of HarperCollins*Publishers*
77–85 Fulham Palace Road
Hammersmith, London W6 8JB

www.harpercollins.co.uk

and *HarperElement* are trademarks
of HarperCollins*Publishers* Ltd

First published by HarperElement 2010

1 3 5 7 9 10 8 6 4 2

© Pea Horsley 2010

Pea Horsley asserts the moral right to
be identified as the author of this work

A catalogue record of this book is
available from the British Library

ISBN 978-0-00-732660-0

Printed and bound in Great Britain by
Clays Ltd, St Ives plc

Mixed Sources
Product group from well-managed
forests and other controlled sources
www.fsc.org Cert no. SW-COC-001806
© 1996 Forest Stewardship Council

FSC is a non-profit international organisation established to promote the
responsible management of the world's forests. Products carrying the FSC
label are independently certified to assure consumers that they come
from forests that are managed to meet the social, economic and
ecological needs of present and future generations.

Find out more about HarperCollins and the environment at
www.harpercollins.co.uk/green

This book is dedicated to Morgan, a pure-bred mutt of questionable beagle heritage.

He changed my life.

Now he may change yours.

Contents

Foreword

FOR AS LONG as I can remember I have wanted to work with animals. So when I stepped out of the Royal Veterinary College, London, in the dim and distant days of 1973, a qualified veterinary surgeon, I had already realized my life's ambition. I had trained for five years, I had letters after my name and I thought I could cure every pet of every disease under the sun. Little did I know that the real learning process was only just beginning.

Within a few years I had become reasonably proficient at the mechanics of being a vet. I could carry out all but the most intricate operations efficiently and speedily, I could prescribe drugs, I could diagnose as well as anybody else. But I began to feel something was missing. There were patients that simply couldn't be diagnosed, despite exhaustive investigations, there were patients for whom drugs had more damaging side-effects than benefits and there were patients that simply refused to respond to treatment that should have worked. It struck me that pets were not little machines that all behaved in the same way to the same treatment. They were living, breathing, sentient beings that sometimes went their own way.

It was at this point that I discovered the alternative world of therapies such as acupuncture, herbal medicine and homoeopathy – a world where the feelings, emotions and character of the patient were equally as important as their physical symptoms. At last I could treat my patients as whole beings rather than as collections of body parts. Within a few years I had closed my practice and opened a centre to treat pets with natural therapies only. Joining me at the centre were other pet therapists – an osteopath, a physiotherapist and a healer.

The healer, Charles Siddle, opened my eyes to a completely new aspect of animal treatment. He just seemed to 'know' what was wrong with pets. When I asked him how, he said, with a twinkle in his eye, 'Oh, they just tell me.'

Around this time I went to a lecture given by the scientist Rupert Sheldrake about a book he had just written, *Dogs That Know When Their Owners Are Coming Home*. Rupert had undertaken months of painstaking work on this subject and proved beyond any reasonable doubt that some dogs really are telepathic and know, amongst other things, exactly when their owners are coming home.

So, if dogs are telepathic and can read our thoughts, why not the other way round? Why shouldn't we be able to read the thoughts of animals and communicate with them?

My own journey of discovery about the treatment of animals from 'veterinary mechanic' to 'holistic therapist' has been endlessly fascinating. Pea Horsley's journey in becoming an animal communicator, from doubting through training to believing to success, has followed the same pattern. This book details that journey. When you have finished it, you may not believe a man can fly, but you'll certainly believe a woman can talk to a rabbit.

Richard Allport,
BVetMed, VetMFHom, MRCVS,
author of *Natural Healthcare for Pets, Heal Your Dog the Natural Way* and *Heal Your Cat the Natural Way*

Acknowledgements

WRITING A BOOK is no longer a solo project where one sits hunched over a battered old computer. This is a collaborative project and I owe much to generous, level-headed friends with an endless supply of energy and humour. Through the many stages of realizing my dream I was helped by them in a number of ways – gentle cajoling, firm insistence, honest commentary, direct intervention, hearts full of kindness and bellies full of laughter.

I'd like to give thanks to Katie Read for her faithful encouragement of my first attempt at a book proposal and her invaluable support during those early stages and Jennie Scott for sniffing out my literary imperfections and laughing, or crying, in all the right places.

A bottomless pit of heartfelt love goes to Judy McGeough for her keen cat-eyed awareness for detail, for lion-hearted encouragement through the challenging moments and above all for understanding the process, and me, without the desire to change either. Judy, this book wouldn't exist without you.

I wish to thank Johanna Town for not thinking I was crazy when I first said I'd been talking to a rabbit and for encouraging my dream in writing this book. My love also goes to Mary Cunningham for adopting me into her family and life-journey support.

Thank you to Zoë King, my literary agent, for believing in this subject and being as excited about this book as I am, to Kate Latham, my editor, for absorbing these stories into her heart, to Lizzie Hutchins, my copy editor, for her amazing eye for detail, to Carole Tonkinson, from HarperCollins, for seeing a future where animal communication can exist in the mainstream alongside other healing modalities for animal well-being, and to everyone from HarperCollins who worked to bring *Heart to Heart* to the bookshelves.

My gratitude extends to all the guardians mentioned in this book who enthusiastically agreed to share their stories in the hope that one of them will not only touch your heart but also inspire and help both you and your animals. Every one of you was an integral part to the writing and I'm grateful for your time, energy and courage in reliving many heartbreaking moments.

My love shines out to the animals who have crossed my path and taught me so much, and to all the animals within these pages who wish to communicate with you heart to heart.

Finally, to two dear four-pawed friends who tenderly hold my heart and soul, Texas and Morgan, this book is a credit to your strength and love.

Introduction

❧ *We Are All Born Intuitive* ❧

LET'S IMAGINE a world where we are born pure and innocent. A world where we are open to anything and everything. A world that is an adventure of discovery from the moment of waking to the moment of sleeping. This world is our world, the only difference is our age – we are babies. For us, everything is possible and the only limitations are those set by those around us, for our imagination is free and wild and we go wherever it takes us. As babies we are naturally telepathic, because we are communicating with life through our senses. How many times have you noticed a baby look wide-mouthed and smiling at a dog walking by wagging his tail? The baby can feel the dog's happiness. If we smile at a baby, she smiles back. If we are upset, she looks concerned. If we are angry and shout, she cries. We don't need to tell her verbally how we are feeling; she is using her senses to receive this information. We continue to use all our senses to understand our interactions until around about the age of seven. Animals continue to use their senses for non-verbal communication all their life.

I discovered animal communication existed for the first time in 2004. I also discovered it's not a gift: everyone can communicate with animals. The only reason the entire human race isn't doing it is because we have been conditioned not to. As we grow up we are taught to ignore our intuition about situations and people. We develop a belief system that is not our own. Our parents, grandparents, teachers and society condition us to trust in their beliefs, until finally we lose touch with our own intuition and rely on everyone else's for guidance.

By tuning back into our own intuition, into our senses, we can open the doorway to inter-species communication. John Wheeler, the physicist, once said, 'Everything must be based on a simple idea. Once we have finally discovered it, it will be so compelling, so beautiful, that we will say to one another, "Yes, how could it have been any different?"' That's how it is with animal communication – it's a simple idea that is so compelling, so beautiful, that once discovered you'll wonder how life could have been like anything other than this.

We're not humanizing animals by listening to their thoughts, we're enabling them to have a voice in a world where they struggle to be heard. We communicate with animals to understand them and to bring them comfort. As we do this, we continue to respect all species and their own laws of nature. This is essential to animals' health and well-being.

Communication with animals is a deep, tender, intuitive and heartfelt method which can bring joy and end suffering.

It can be a step towards a world where animals are seen as equals and treated with respect.

This is my gentle introduction to the subject of animal communication, told with the help of the animals with whom I shared my journey. It is my hope that you, too, will step out on this path and find that life is as surprising and exciting as it was when you were younger.

Empower yourself by venturing beyond the boundary of your own current experience, of what you have always believed to be true in your life, and prepare to join everyone who has contributed to placing this book in your hands on a wondrous journey of seeing animals in all their glory.

Author's Note

I HAVE WRITTEN this book with the intention it will be healing to both you and your non-human loved ones. My hope is that these true-life stories will open your eyes, free your minds and bring you comfort in your grief or suffering.

I owe much to the truth and integrity of the animal guardians who joined me in retelling their experiences with their animal loved ones. A few characters have been disguised, but the vast majority of the names of animals and guardians have remained the same, to honour them and pay tribute to them for their valued contribution.

Animal communication, however valuable, is not a substitute for the expert diagnosis of a trusted veterinarian. If you feel your animals are unwell, please seek out a medical professional who is caring, compassionate and respectful to you and your animals.

CHAPTER 1

Intuition Ignited

SITTING BOLT upright on my uncomfortable plastic chair, arms folded over my chest, legs crossed and no doubt a scowl on my face, I was wondering what on Earth was happening here. I didn't believe a word of it. A rather dubious-looking man in casual jeans and a sweater was trying to tell me we could talk to animals!

At the time I was working as company stage manager at the Comedy Theatre in London's West End on a play called *The Old Masters* directed by Harold Pinter. Working for 15 years in the theatre, sourcing props, calculating wages, organizing schedules, running dress rehearsals, looking after the company and making sure everything went smoothly, especially on press night, I considered myself a practical and sensible person, not airy-fairy like. Yet here I was sitting listening to *Doctor Doolittle*-type stories.

So how did I get here? Let me take you back to where it all started and I'll explain. In the very beginning my journey began with cats.

❧ Cat 'Grooming' ❧

All my life I have been a *huge* cat fanatic. As a young child I grew up with a cat called Pixie, a no-nonsense minute dynamo. Her beautiful swirls of caramel, coffee and chocolate fooled the unwary to believing she was gooey and soft, but in reality she was more Joanna Lumley in spurs. Her original owners, our neighbours, often left her alone whilst they went on holiday without arranging for her meals and care, and Pixie checked out my family while they were away and decided to adopt us. I remember my parents and the neighbours having a bit of a heated argument about it until finally my dad said, 'Pixie should be allowed to make up her own mind where she wants to live.' And she did. She immediately packed her bags and moved in with us. Not long after, her old family moved away. They didn't even come by to say goodbye to her.

Pixie's favourite sunbathing spot became the bed my mum made out of an old veggie box and some soft towels, positioned on the top shelf in the greenhouse. Years later, just before we buried her in our garden, my mum cut off a small piece of her fur, which I sellotaped into my 'Favourite Things' notebook, along with one of her whiskers. I was upset, but not distraught. Through her independent spirit and her fierce protection of her personal space, Pixie helped me to learn these qualities, and also, I feel, subconsciously, she taught me that we all have the right to be cared for and loved.

Then Winston, my second cat, entered my teenage life and promptly took it over. The first night he arrived home he draped his large butterscotch body over my lap and we fell madly and deeply in love. I was about 13 at the time and he was my first boyfriend. He was adopted from a rescue centre in Warwickshire, but he didn't carry the marks of a mistreated cat, he was a laid-back kinda guy who gave off an air of Italian Romeo entwined with Mafia boss. I saw him a bit like a lion who was very comfortable in his own skin.

The hardest part about leaving home to attend Bristol Old Vic Theatre School was leaving Winston behind. He always knew when I was upset and would find me to offer affection and just be with me during my sadness. He'd also meet me from school, having an uncanny ability to know when to sit and wait for me at the top of the road. We developed a friendship where he was my comforter, my rock, and we grew so close, we had an unspoken understanding of one another, like an inner knowing.

As often as I could, I went home especially to see him and I thought about him all the time. When he began to lose weight and became sick, those trips back home were heartbreaking, for I never knew whether I would see him again. Then one day I received a call and my parents told me it was time to put him to sleep. Once I'd put the phone down I cried out loud in agonizing pain. It felt as if my stomach was being ripped out. When Winston passed over I was utterly heartbroken and it took a long time for the pain to subside. I was 29 before I was in a position to welcome a new cat into my life.

I never thought for a minute another cat would be able to touch my heart like Winston, but at that time I hadn't met Texas. He captured my heart the moment he bolted out of his wired-fronted cage at London's Battersea Dogs' and Cats' Home and rubbed his tiny six-month body slam-dunk against my legs. He was a miniature tiger with mellow gold, ginger and cream stripes, a soft pink nose, yellow-green eyes and gleaming ivory-white whiskers. He was stunning, really friendly and the sexiest cat I'd ever met – it was a done deal.

I now feel these cats were grooming me, teaching me and preparing me all my life for the moment when I would consciously realize humans and animals could communicate with one another using an intuitive language. But, to my surprise, it took a *dog* to make me understand inter-species communication was possible and that I could learn to talk to animals.

🐾 *Morgan Arrives* 🐾

It all began for me when I adopted my first dog from the Mayhew Animal Home: an eight-year old scruffy mutt of questionable beagle heritage whom I named Morgan.

Morgan looks like an older version of one of the best-known trademarks in the world, 'His Master's Voice' – a terrier with a cocked head listening intently to his master's voice coming from a gramophone horn. He has a broken coat of both rough and smooth grungy white hair with velvet soft beagle chestnut ears that invite you to stroke them and a smooth chestnut face-mask streaked with a terrier flash up between his eyes. His almond-shaped eyes with heavy black eyeliner, black play-dough nose and thick black lips give him an almost clown-like appearance. Underneath his tummy hair he has Parson Russell terrier brown splodges and he has a thick mane of hair over his shoulders.

He was lying on the floor of the admin. offices when I first met him, cushioned by a thick duvet. I knelt down and he welcomed me by rolling onto his back and lifting up his paw, inviting me to stroke his chest. My partner Jo and I jointly decided he was 'the one' because he had such a gentle face. When I looked at him there was also another quality I couldn't put my finger on, which seemed to melt my heart, making me feel safe to be in his company. Initially we were looking for a female springer spaniel, but when we spotted Morgan we fell in love with his face and felt it would be easier for an older dog to fit in with our work commitments and for us to meet his needs.

The truth is I was concerned about getting a dog. It was Jo's idea, not mine. I was madly and deeply in love with Texas and concerned he'd be scared or angry if we brought another animal into the home. Texas liked being the centre of attention and my biggest fear was that he'd rehome himself. I also had a childhood fear. When I was a young girl, around nine or ten, I was chased off a farm by a pack of Jack Russells. I was terri-fied as they barked and ran after me, biting down on my ankles. This fear was multiplied when someone's stocky

Labrador was let off the lead and came charging over to me, barking aggressively.

This fear of dogs made it impossible for me to walk anywhere that dogs were free to roam. Where I lived in Stratford-on-Avon there was a short cut into town down a disused tramline. It was right next to the 'rec' and some people would walk their dogs along there. If I saw a dog coming towards me off the lead, fear would rise from my belly, my chest would feel as if it was caving in, making it hard to breathe, and tears would try to spring from my eyes. Of course, the dogs would sense my fear and that would make the whole situation worse because then they'd start to bark at me or raise their hackles and growl. I'd have no choice: I'd have to return the way I'd come then go the long route, my legs weak and quivering. Inviting a dog into the safety of my home was quite a large step for me.

Morgan arrived and the ceiling didn't fall in. Though Texas was not impressed by our new choice of companion and ran away whenever he came close. And in the first few days of getting to know Morgan, he bit my nose. Well, that's what I thought, and I burst into tears as the moment triggered all the years I had held on to my fear of dogs attacking me. It was a shock having a dog's face and teeth right in my face. For a moment I thought, *He's going to have to go back. This isn't going to work.* Later, when I knew Morgan better, I realized he was just being affectionate. He hadn't bit me, he'd just given me a friendly nibble. To this day Morgan has remembered that moment and occasionally, when he spontaneously goes to give my nose a nibble, he'll suddenly stop himself and lower his head in shame. I still feel bad about this and say sorry for the way I reacted to him.

In those early days Morgan would lie in his bed and I would sit on the floor next to him giving him a gentle stroke. I didn't know him and he didn't know me, yet intuitively this felt the right thing to do. I wanted to comfort him. I had a hunch that he was sad but I put this down to the obvious reasons: he was in a strange place, with people he didn't know, and he had no idea whether he was staying or whether this was just another temporary arrangement and he'd soon be carted off somewhere else.

But after the initial settling-in period rescued animals need, I became aware that Morgan's sadness was not going away. He looked miserable lying in his brand-new luxury fleece bed and when we were out walking he'd bark obsessively at old men with walking sticks, whether they were near or far. I thought maybe I was doing something wrong. I knew cats, but I wasn't an experienced dog owner. Or dog guardian, as I prefer to be called now.

When the Mayhew Animal Home e-mailed to say they were holding an animal communication workshop which would help me to get to know my animal *even better*, I knew I had to go along. I can't really explain logically why I went; it was just a gut feeling. I had to go, even though I hadn't looked into other ways of helping Morgan – I hadn't called in a behaviourist and I would never have considered an animal healer in those days. I just didn't think of or follow any other options.

❧ *The Lightbulb Workshop* ❧

So that is what brought me across a cold blue London, in the autumn of 2004, to sit in an uncomfortable plastic chair listening to *Doctor Doolittle* stories. When I imagined everyone else was having lazy Sunday lie-ins and croissants and getting their fix of *The Archers*.

Twenty people, mostly women, were sitting round in a large circle, with the teacher at the front of the room. He began to tell us how he'd found he could talk to animals. He said he'd realized he'd had this amazing magical power since he was a child, and as a teenager he'd often speak to horses and have conversations with them. *What have I got myself into?* I thought. *He can talk to animals? No, that's not right: no one can talk to animals, except Doctor Doolittle of course.* Then he shared an emotional story of how his miraculous gift had helped a distraught animal and it wasn't long before 19 people were crying.

And then there was me. *Forgive me if I'm wrong, but isn't this man telling us he actually speaks to animals, and, er, hears what they say back to him?* It took all my will-power to stop myself from walking out. I was astonished, soaked head to foot in disbelief, yet everyone else seemed taken in. They must have been bewitched when they came in. Was I the only one who didn't believe this con man?

By the time we'd reached lunchtime I was hungry and grumpy. I was even more sceptical than when I'd walked in at nine o'clock. The morning had been dominated by animal stories and a couple of 'getting in touch with your senses' exercises, but we hadn't even glimpsed a cat or a dog, let alone talked to one.

During lunch, I made a beeline for the teacher. 'We've got an awful lot to cover if we're going to be speaking with animals this afternoon,' I said.

He just smiled and carried on eating his vegetarian scotch egg.

Shortly after lunch I was pleased to see my words had had some effect. We were put into pairs and told to swap the photos that we'd brought of our animals at home. So my partner had a photo of my cat, Texas, and I had a photo of her … well, I didn't know what. I was given the photo face down and told to guess what animal was in the picture.

How the heck am I supposed to know? I felt foolish and awkward. As much as I didn't believe in all this hocus-pocus, I didn't want to make a fool of myself in front of such a large group of strangers, and because my childhood passion had always been animals, there was a part of me that was curious to try it for myself. All my inner demons flew out of my mind and began stabbing me with their spears. *What if I'm the only one here who can't do this? I'll make an idiot of myself. I don't want to get it wrong. It's not real.* I took a deep breath and fought my demons: *I've got nothing to lose. I've paid my money now. I'm here, so I might as well give it a go. What if he really can talk to animals? I want to do that too! And I'm probably never going to see these people again anyway.*

I looked at the white back of the photo and scribbled a word on my notepad. It was the first word that came into my mind – I just heard it, almost as though it had been whispered in my ear: 'Rabbit.'

When I turned the photo over, I found myself staring into the soft shiny eyes of a deep rich sepia-coloured rabbit. *Lucky guess. It was hardly likely to be a giraffe*. The demons had returned, spears at the ready.

My partner told me this rabbit was called Mister Butch. Then the teacher instructed us to ask our animal a few rudimentary questions: 'What's his favourite food?' 'What's his favourite activity?' 'Where does he like to sleep?' 'Who is he in love with?'

The room fell silent as everyone knuckled down. Everyone except me, that is. My mind was racing with doubt, my demons were gaining ground and the opposition was retreating. As I looked down at Mister Butch, my internal dialogue went like this:

'I've been told to talk to you, but you can't hear me. You can't hear me because you're a photo, a photo of a rabbit, and rabbits can't talk. Let alone photos of rabbits. You can't hear me, can you, because rabbits *don't* talk.'

'Who do you think is listening to you?'

I heard this response like a voice inside me, but it was a male voice and it wasn't happy, it was confrontational. Was the rabbit in the photo really talking to me?

'Did you just speak to me?' I asked warily in my mind as I looked at Mister Butch in the photo.

'Yeah! I can hear you, all right!' came that voice again.

Butterflies were fluttering around my stomach. For the first time I wondered whether I could believe what I was hearing internally.

'You can really hear me? As I talk to you, you hear me?'

Yeah, I said it already: I can hear you. Who the hell do you think is listening?'

I took a moment to gather myself. *They're starting to get to me. All this talk has started to have some strange kind of effect.* Yet a part of me really wanted it to be true because I really loved animals and, more importantly, I had a sad dog at home and I wanted to make his life happier. I decided to get the most out of the afternoon.

'OK, Mister Butch, if you can hear me, tell me what your favourite food is,' I quizzed.

'Leaves.'

I scribbled it on my pad. Then I heard the negative voice in my mind again: *Well! If that wasn't obvious!*

I carried on. 'And what's your environment like?'

In my mind I could see a picture of a plush lawn, then the image changed and I saw a bed, and then it changed again and I saw a two-seater sofa. I wrote it all down.

'Are you in love with anyone right now?'

There was another brief picture, this time of an espresso-coloured rabbit. It came and went ever so fast.

'And what's your favourite activity?'

There was another flash of that sofa.

Quite a long time had passed whilst I was doing this exercise, but it felt like just a few minutes. The moment came to share the information I'd written down with Mister Butch's guardian. Even though I felt as if I'd made up every word of it, I went through each response.

My partner told me some of the things didn't make sense, but some of them were correct. Mister Butch's big love was an espresso-coloured rabbit and apparently I'd really tuned into his strong character: he was an impatient rabbit with atti-tude. As it turned out, he'd also done this before: he'd commu-nicated with our teacher. No wonder I'd been able to sense his disapproval as I'd groped about in disbelief – he was an old pro. My partner even elaborated on the image I'd seen when I'd asked the question: 'What's your favourite activity?' She told me Mister Butch would come inside and sit on her sofa at the same time every Saturday evening. He would expect the television to be on and switched to his favourite programme, *You've Been Framed.* When we shared our communications with the entire group, the other students thought this snippet was hilarious and our teacher was even able to corroborate the story: he'd been to visit Mister Butch at his home and witnessed his TV addiction for himself.

As outlandish yet wonderful as this experience seemed, I still found it hard to believe that I had communicated with a rabbit using a photograph. Let alone a rabbit that watched TV. I thought his guardian was just being kind and encouraging, and maybe it was the law of averages that had produced a couple of accuracies.

Then it was my partner's turn to tell me everything she'd received in response from my cat, Texas. This complete stranger started to describe the layout of my living-room, the colour of my sofa and Texas' favourite place to sit in the garden. How could she know this? How could she get all this from a photo?

And if this complete stranger was able to receive accurate information from Texas, was I, maybe, just maybe, also receiving accurate information from Mister Butch?

My God, this is really happening. I've just talked to a rabbit. From his photo.

It was the most miraculous idea: *animals can talk and we can hear them.*

My body and mind felt in conflict with what I'd experienced during the day and my belief system prior to it. In a daze I drove home, feeling excited, awestruck and completely over-whelmed. I felt that I was sailing out into the ocean without a paddle, surrounded by the deep blue sea. I didn't know which way I was heading or how far I would travel. I didn't know how many fathoms of undiscovered secrets lay beneath me. These were unchartered waters. I began to think of how my friends might respond if I were to tell them I'd just had a conversation with a rabbit.

And yet, even though I had this logical fear, I couldn't help but question my sceptical beliefs. The idea of being able to communicate with animals was changing my perception of reality. It was changing how I viewed animals. *If people were to realize they could talk to animals, just think how much happier animals could be. They'd be able to tell us what they wanted and how they felt. If everyone learned to talk to animals*

– my God, that could change everything. Animals everywhere could be recognized as feeling and thinking creatures who can make their own decisions and form their own relationships. I was getting so excited, but then I had a thought that brought me crashing down to reality: *What about all the animals behind bars in zoos?* I suddenly felt a heavy weight in the pit of my stomach. *And all the animals in shelters with no one to love them and make them feel special – what must they be feeling?* My chest heaved and my eyes filled with tears as I thought of cosmetic testing, the fur industry and vivisection.

This discovery didn't feel quite so delightful anymore. Joy had been replaced by unbearable anguish. And that's when I realized the journey into animal communication might not be so easy after all. It was coupled with enormous responsibility. The joy of communicating with animals would always go hand in hand with the anguish of how my fellow human beings would treat them. I realized that during my communications with animals, I would hear what they thought and feel what they felt. On the one hand, that would be their loving connection with people. Yet, travelling down the same path, I'd also feel all their suffering: their feelings of sadness, confusion, betrayal and loneliness, even their anger.

In just one day I felt my life had changed and I was looking at the world with fresh eyes.

❧ *Returning Home* ❧

At home I had the daunting task of telling my partner about the day's events. How do you tell someone you've just been conversing with a rabbit? There are no manuals to advise and I'd be surprised if the answer can be revealed by a web search. And I was still finding it hard to understand what had happened myself.

Jo had made us some tea and we were relaxing in the living-room drinking it when she asked me how the workshop had gone. I laughed nervously.

'OK,' I said.

Then there was a palatable silence as I tried to grasp the right words. I just didn't know how to tell her. I decided the only way forward was just to say it.

'I think I've just been talking to a rabbit. I think I can talk to animals.'

I held my breath, waiting for her reaction.

She looked across at Morgan and raised her eyebrows, then looked back at me and smiled. 'Well, that's going to be an interesting hobby,' she said. Little did she, or I, know at this point that it was going to evolve into something much greater. Then she added, 'How do you know? Give me proof.'

I told her the details I'd received and that some of them had made sense. I said I didn't know *how* it had happened, it just had. I also told her that a complete stranger had talked to Texas and described the colour of our sofa and his favourite lookout post in the garden. How could that be possible?

'Wow,' she said, 'that sounds amazing.' Then, without a moment's hesitation, 'What did the rabbit say?'

I should have known Jo would react positively. She had always loved animals – dogs being her favourite – and I think that connection helps you see there is more to an animal than sit, beg and roll over. Since that moment I have always been supported on my journey into animal communication. I am lucky in that way.

That evening I knelt on the floor in front of Morgan and looked into his deep espresso-coloured eyes. He looked straight back at me and I had the feeling he was saying, 'So now you know.' The veil had been lifted and I could see him clearly, not only as a feeling and thinking dog but also with the realization we could connect with each other on this intuitive, heartfelt level for even deeper and clearer understanding.

❧ Listening ❧

I now know that animal communication is not so much about talking as listening; it's about being a receptive vessel. I now realize I'd been subconsciously preparing for this. Over the years I'd been drawn to jobs where it was important to listen. Before I began to communicate with animals I volunteered on a helpline. Every weekend for approximately three months I attended training, culminating in a mock-up practical test at the end. The tutors would only allow you in the phone room if they felt you were ready and once there you received a buddy who would give you one-to-one support and guidance in the first few weeks. After I'd finished working in the theatre in the evening I'd head over to the helpline headquarters and stay up all night manning the phone. The 'graveyard' night shift was very unpopular, so I'd often be there on my own. People rang with a whole range of problems, some extremely upsetting, some shocking, some traumatic, and then there were people who just needed to talk to someone who would listen without their own agenda or any judgement.

Looking back now, this provided the groundwork of how it feels to truly listen and I am sure it was one of the building blocks for communicating with animals. And of course I had worked with actors and creative types in the theatre, which meant I had learned to juggle different personalities within a pressured profession where deadlines were absolute.

❧ *Sharing My Discovery* ❧

Sharing my discovery wasn't easy. I was nervous about telling my friends. I felt awkward saying the words, 'I've discovered I can talk to animals,' sort of embarrassed, and also scared of how they would respond.

I began by telling two close friends whom I'd known for the longest time. One of them, also called Jo, took a little while to get her head around it, but at the same time felt there was no reason why it shouldn't be possible. She said, 'I think when you've had a pet you feel really close to, it doesn't seem such an alien idea that someone would find a way of communicating with animals.'

But my other friend from theatre school, Caroline, went silent on the phone. She still doesn't understand it.

Dinner parties, and most social events like birthdays and weddings, have since become a great adventure. Sometimes I'll be asked what I do and I'll tell someone and the brick wall will immediately come up or their eyes will glaze over or they'll be speechless. Others might say, 'Really? Glass of wine?' then make a hasty retreat, never to return. There are some nights when I've received a handful of these types of reactions and I've been tempted to tell people I'm a mortician instead, or a fire fighter, or a pole dancer, or even an astronaut. A lot of people use humour because they don't know what to say. On the other hand some will immediately believe me and have a million questions, or else pin me in a corner, desperate to resolve the ins and outs of their cat's inappropriate toileting. Largely, people are intrigued and want to know all about it and how it works.

The most popular question is, of course, 'What did the rabbit say?'

❧ *Resolving Morgan's Sadness* ❧

I was so intrigued by the thought that I might be able to talk to animals I immediately signed up for a second workshop. During this experience I felt excited and found my communications with animals had a better flow of accuracy. I was able to give the colour of an animal's bed, where it was positioned and even whom the animal lived with. It was at this second workshop that I discovered my life's purpose. I know that might sound like a cliché, but it's true. That is how it happened. It wasn't a logical decision – I just knew in my heart that I had discovered what I wanted to do for the rest of my life. It felt right.

So then I felt confident enough to concentrate on the reason why I'd started all this in the first place: Morgan. I wanted to understand why he looked sad and so I spent a long time talking to him. He was lying in his bed in my light, homely living-room and I was sitting on the wooden floor in front of him. I began by asking him whether he liked his food.

'It's OK,' he said.

'And do you feel you receive enough exercise?' I asked gently, looking into his watery brown eyes.

'I suppose. It's a bit boring. I'd like some bones, something to crunch,' came a downhearted voice that melted my heart and sparked worry lines across my brow. I wondered whether it was me. Maybe he didn't like me?

'Do you like me, Morgan?'

'Yes.'

Then he decided to bite on the duvet in his bed, like a child sucks on a 'diddy'.

We'd reached the point where I had to ask him: 'Why are you sad, sweetheart?'

After much patient cajoling, Morgan slowly revealed the background to his feelings. He showed me an image of an old man with a walking stick and I felt guilt – Morgan felt he was letting the old man down. Then there was an image of an old woman sitting in a high-backed armchair with Morgan lying at her feet. She appeared very smiley and gentle, and I felt she had now passed over and was in spirit. Then I heard the words, 'Look after my husband when I'm gone.' She was looking at Morgan when she said it. I was hearing these words in my mind, but the voice wasn't mine, it was older, softer and slower. I could feel the love Morgan felt for the woman and the love she felt for him. They adored one another.

Morgan told me they were his previous owners. As I looked into his eyes, I tried to tune into the old man again and saw an image of him standing in a small galley kitchen. He seemed flustered and unable to cope. He was holding a walking stick, which reminded me of the old men with walking sticks that Morgan would bark at on our walks. As Morgan shared his secret I could sense how confused he was feeling. Tuning back into the image of the man, I got the feeling he'd been taken into care after his wife had died. That must have been why Morgan had been taken to death row.

I'd learned on the workshop that one way to resolve emotional upset between people and animals, and even animals and animals, was to invite them into the same space. I began by imagining a bright safe space with a wooden door, and while I looked into Morgan's eyes, I invited the spirit of the old lady to enter and take a seat in the high-backed chair I'd created for her.

Once she'd settled, I invited Morgan to enter the space. He walked in, body tense, refusing to look at the old lady, keeping his eyes permanently fixed to the floor. 'Physical Morgan' still lay in bed, but 'energetic Morgan' came into the safe space. The feelings of guilt and remorse were palatable.

I invited the lady to take over. She turned to face Morgan and told him how much she loved him. This caused him to sink even lower into the floor, as if he wanted the earth to open and swallow him up.

'He couldn't take care of himself anymore,' the lady said to his back. 'He needed a very special home. He wasn't able to take you with him, that's why you were parted.'

Tears started to trickle down my cheeks as I was feeling what Morgan was feeling. He was listening transfixed to what she was saying and had begun to cry.

'It's not your fault. You did nothing wrong,' she said.

For the first time, Morgan turned round and looked up at her, a pleading look in his eyes.

She continued, 'No, love. You didn't let me down. You did your job brilliantly and I am very proud of you.'

I burst into tears as I felt a huge wave of emotional relief sweep over Morgan. I cried and cried as he let go of the burden he'd been carrying with him.

But the old lady didn't stop there. 'I want you to move on now,' she said. 'You kept your promise; you looked after him so well. Now you're with a new family and I want you to look after them. This is your new job: to be with this family.'

In the safe place I'd created, Morgan began to prance joyously around, his mouth smiling wide open. It was as though a weight of responsibility had been removed from his shoulders.

I thanked the lady, then I thanked Morgan for being brave enough to enter in the first place and finally I dissolved the picture and brought my awareness back to the room.

Once I was calmer, I looked into the eyes of my beautiful dog lying in his bed in front of me and said to him, 'I want you to live with my family now. We want you to be with us and I promise you we will love you, maybe not in the same way as your previous family, but we'll do our best to love you just as much.'

He visibly relaxed and I thought his eyes began to sparkle.

What was more remarkable was Texas' behaviour. The very same day, he stopped running away from Morgan. When I asked him why he didn't appear to be scared of him anymore, he replied simply, 'He's decided he's staying.' Texas now viewed him as part of the family rather than an outsider. Even my friends could see a difference in Morgan and the way Texas now accepted him.

CHAPTER 2

Practice, Practice, Practice

FROM THAT DAY on I spent every waking moment reading up on the subject of animal communication and badgered my friends to let me practise with their animals, or their friends' animals, or their neighbours' animals. I also joined animal-related web forums.

Soon word got out that I was willing to offer a free communication to anyone who wanted one and all they needed to do in return was verify the details I gave them, so I could see how I was progressing and learn from my successes and failures. I was always honest and upfront, explaining that I was still a student and that I might not always get it right. I asked the recipient to take responsibility for the communication and whether they chose to ignore it or take notice of it was up to them. If there was anything medically wrong with their animal I always asked them to seek the advice of a trusted veterinarian.

❧ *Street-Cool Sammy* ❧

On Saturday 4 December 2004, I recorded my first practice case study in a large orange hardback notebook. To begin with, I was attempting it without a photo of the animal. All I knew was that the animal was a cat who shared his or her life with a woman called Chloë, who was the casting agent of a friend of mine. I didn't even have the cat's name.

I decided to gather some impressions, details that Chloë could verify. I sat in my favourite comfy chair and tried to tune into the cat. I imagined I was connecting with him or her by silently asking 'the cat of Chloë' to come forward and show him or herself. Then I saw a quick picture in my mind – the image of a deep rich brown cat. I sensed the general character of this cat and wrote down a few words: 'gentle', 'loving', 'weary', 'tired', 'needs rest'. I asked what he or she was called and heard 'Molly', 'Polly' and 'Dolly'.

A few days later Chloë sent me a photo and I found myself looking into the eyes of a deep rich brown cat. I gave myself a tick in my notebook for getting that right. Chloë still hadn't included a name, so I persevered without one.

'Please tell me what you're called,' I said, as I held the cat's photo in my hands.

'Frank. Frankie,' came a deep male voice inside my head.

'Is that right? You're called Frankie?' My impression had been that this cat was female.

'No, but I'd prefer this name, I'd rather be called Frank or Frankie. I need more street-cred. But it's too late now,' came the deep booming voice.

I'd begun to get a better sense of his character and wrote down a few more words to describe him: 'bright', intelligent', 'relaxed', 'solid', 'Other cats leave him alone', 'He has quite a presence', 'A bit of a gangster, wouldn't mess with him, but it's all front', 'He has a big heart and adores his mum.'

From his comments it appeared that this puss wasn't under house arrest and liked to patrol his neighbourhood. 'How do you leave your garden?' I asked him. 'Which direction do you like to head in?'

Suddenly I saw an image of a brick wall on the left of a tiny-looking garden and a ladder – a wooden cat-width ladder, with rungs cat-stride deep, at an easy-to-climb 45-degree angle.

'She's made a hole and given me steps,' said the male voice. 'I can't jump that high anymore.'

At the weekend I caught up with Chloë on the phone to check what her cat was called before I continued communicating using her questions. 'He's called Sammy,' she told me.

'Molly', 'Polly', 'Dolly' and 'Frankie' had a vaguely similar sound to Sammy, but I knew there was room for improvement, and quite clearly I'd mistaken him as female.

'Chloë, have you made a hole in the brick wall on the left side of your back garden?' I asked.

'Yes, I have … How did you know that?' she said, astonished.

'And did you also put a wooden cat-ladder there?' I continued.

There was a gasp and a moment's silence on the other end of the phone, then Chloë said, 'That's remarkable, Pea. Did Sammy tell you that? How could you have known that? I had to give him a ladder, he was finding it harder to make the jump and he loves to explore.'

I was flabbergasted too. As much as I'd hoped it was true, because it seemed way too quirky for me to invent, the negativity inside me had said, *No you're just making it up, you've got a fanciful imagination, cats don't need ladders to exit their gardens. For goodness sake, he's a cat!*

A week later I was sitting in Chloë's living room delivering the rest of Sammy's communication as he sat next to me on the sofa. 'He never does that with people he's not met before,' she said. 'It's as if he knows you.'

During home visits animals often give gentle encouragement by climbing onto my lap or settling close by. Sometimes dogs lean into me or uncharacteristically make a big fuss as though we've met before. Birds soon relax and let me close too. Animals seem to do this for a number of reasons, mainly, I feel, to give their guardian a clear sign of their approval of the process, but also as a supportive 'nod' to me that I am on the right track.

❧ *Bluesy Makes Demands* ❧

Another early practice case was with a cat called Bluesy. She is a tiny caramel and chocolate swirled feline who rules over the home of Lynn and Sandra and a 66lb golden retriever called Saffie. Those who know her well may feel there is a leopard inside this tiny fragile body – her spirit is strong and her green-tea eyes cut into you with a no-nonsense 'Don't mess with me' stare. This formidable character rules supreme from her throne room on the first floor at the rear of the house overlooking the garden. This is 'Bluesy's room' and her throne is an old armchair in the corner. Bluesy is very particular about her space, disliking changes, but is generous enough to allow her large Goldilocks companion to occupy the floor nearby.

At the start of this story I was chummier with Saffie, who brought her two human companions along to join Morgan and me on treks around the common. Lynn is in her fifth decade and the fittest woman I know. Under her baggy clothing she disguises muscle tone any woman, or man, would die for and has unquestionable strength. Sandra is a little bit younger, with neat blonde bobbed hair and a caring nature. Both women are successful in their individual careers within the NHS.

One day we were all walking together when Lynn and Sandra told me their news: the vet had diagnosed Bluesy with a small growth in one of her kidneys and she had transformed from the bossy boots of the house into a quiet skin and bones waif. The veterinary diagnosis had arrived: 'If you wish to know what type of tumour it is, we will need to investigate, but we need to consider the worst.'

Lynn and Sandra were devastated, trying to come to terms with the notion of losing their 16-year-old *tour de force*. They decided not to put Bluesy through any investigations, given her age.

I was still only practising animal communication at this point, but when I offered my help, Lynn and Sandra were keen to know whether there was anything Bluesy needed to make her more comfortable.

When I connected with Bluesy, distantly, linking in through her photo, I heard a strong, clear voice. She was keen to be heard. Even though her body was weak, her spirit was as strong and as acerbic as ever. She wasn't interested in talking about the colour of her chair or how she felt about any treatment, she wanted to get her shopping list together. Bluesy had demands.

One of the first images I received from her was of a pad on a chair. Then I felt a warm sensation in my own body and she said, just in case the 'stupid human' hadn't got the message: '*Heat pad.*'

I met up with Lynn and Sandra in our favourite pub and, nervously over a pint, began to read back the information from Bluesy in my notepad. I had only discovered animal communication a couple of months earlier, so this was very early on in my experience. I described Bluesy's character traits and they agreed I had her spot on. I described her room and favourite chair, which I didn't know anything about, her status in the house and her relationship with Saffie and each of them. Then I went on to share the two pieces of information Bluesy really wanted to get across.

'She says she wants a heat pad,' I offered. 'She pictured a pad on her seat and I felt the sensation of warmth. She's cold and would like more warmth.'

'Yes,' responded Lynn, in a very matter-of-fact way. 'We've been talking about getting her a heat pad.'

'That's amazing,' said Sandra. We were talking about it only the other day. She's so small and fragile now; we've been worried she might be cold. Well, we'll get her a heat pad. If that's what Bluesy wants then that's what she will have.

'She's asking for one more thing,' I continued, confident now that they were happy to follow Bluesy's wishes. 'She would like fresh food. She pictured chicken and I tasted tuna too. She's fed up with dry food and wants a change.'

'OK, all right. Full of demands, isn't she?!' said Sandra.

Straight away Bluesy was given her heat pad and from first thing in the morning to last thing in the evening, as well as all through the night, she stayed on it, except for the odd trip downstairs for food and a comfort break in the garden. It was a British winter and the weather was miserable and cold.

It was a week or so later that I heard the whole story. It turned out that the heat pad had arrived really quickly, but the food change hadn't materialized straight away. So Bluesy had taken things into her own four paws and gone on hunger strike. She had refused to eat anything put in front of her. Until the tuna arrived, followed swiftly by the chicken.

Since that day Bluesy has eaten with an appetite of which a horse would be proud. She is regularly cooked fresh chicken and every day it disappears into her belly. It has been over five years since her fated prognosis and she has blossomed into a beauty, with lustrous fur you constantly wish to run your hands through. Not that you would dare. Her vet is still able to feel the lump and it is slowly getting bigger, yet, as the vet confirms, 'It doesn't seem to bother her.' Bluesy is full of herself: lording over her servants, screeching commands as she parades around her palace, sometimes during the early hours of the morning. She comes and goes as she pleases and bags the best spot on the sofa every time. She now has two feeding stations and receives room service daily. She is in command and deliriously happy. While life is this good, why would you want to leave? Bluesy is now 21 years old and still in power.

❧ *The Blowfly Mission* ❧

I was taking a little time out, warming my skin and enjoying the silence as I sat in my inner-city garden. I'd just finished a communication with a cat. Texas was soaking up the sun's rays too from his self-made indentation in the uncut grass.

Something caught my attention, causing me to glance over to my left. There on my hand stood a metallic green fly with bristly black legs. His six feet stuck to my skin in between my fine blonde hairs. I stared into two overlarge maroon-coloured eyes.

'Hello,' I said out loud to him.

Even though I thought he'd fly off, he stayed there, as if rooted to my hand, waiting. Then a thought entered my mind: *I wonder if this fly can hear me?*

It was my first attempt at communication with an insect, let alone a fly, and I wondered how I could be sure we were really connected. After a moment's consideration I came up with an idea.

'OK, Fly, please show me you can understand me by flying around the parasol at this table then coming back to rest on my hand again,' I said silently.

Without a second's hesitation the fly vanished into the air. I saw him ascend anti-clockwise around the silver parasol then come to land on my left hand.

'Pouf!' I exhaled. 'That's pretty impressive.' I looked into the deep red eyes facing me. 'Can you do it again?'

My new friend took off, the sunlight gleaming through his fragile translucent wings. Again he flew anti-clockwise around the parasol and came to rest on my left hand. Both times anti-clockwise. Both times the left hand. Was this a coincidence?

This time I looked into the big eyes of my little friend in amazement and admiration. Not only did he appear to be receiving my telepathic communication, he was also choosing to act on it.

Still not quite believing it, I asked him a third time, 'Please fly around the parasol one more time for me and I promise you I will never question that animal communication is possible again.'

Quick as a flash, he was off, up into the air and flying anti-clockwise around the parasol then coming in to land on my left hand again. In the silence he looked up at me expectantly, as if he was waiting for my reaction.

'Incredible! Thank you!' I said, astonished, full of a new sense of appreciation of flies.

A split-second later he was up, off and out of sight.

'Bye,' I said as I watched the fly ambassador leave. It felt as if his job was completed and he'd moved straight on to the next mission.

It took me a while to really let this experience sink in. Here was a common fly who had rested on my hand and instead of flying off had stayed. This tiny insect with his supposedly tiny brain had done something amazing: he'd listened and decided to do what I'd asked him – he'd flown round the parasol a staggering *three* times. I started to look at insects, especially flies, in a new light and I wondered what else they were capable of.

This experience only happened once. It was a special moment between us. But at this point on my animal communication journey it felt like a blessing to be shown so clearly that even the tiny species are capable of inter-species communication. More significantly for me, the fly ambassador had helped silence my sceptical mind.

Now I have a much more respectful view of flies. If they come into my house, rather than thinking of ways to eliminate them, I just open a door or window and ask them to leave. I've found this method works nearly every time.

❧ Mice Matters ❧

It was a cold day in February when I became aware I had squatters. Every time I opened the understairs cupboard to retrieve the vacuum or a recycling bag I was struck with *l'eau de mus musculus*. That would be mouse poop to you and me. The little darlings had left black droppings all over the brown carpet, under the shelving unit and around the recycling box. I would sweep them up, but before long the whole area would be covered in their little presents again.

Straight away it was obvious why they'd decided on this particular hidey-hole: it was where I kept the pet food. And despite the industrial-strength plastic casing, there were tiny mouse-sized holes all along the bottom of the bag. It was freezing outside and probably very difficult to locate enough food. Yet this wasn't making my life any easier – a family of mice can leave a lot of droppings.

One day my suspicion was confirmed by a sighting. I opened the door and heard movement coming from one of the food bags. Maybe the mouse was so hungry he'd forgotten to listen out for the human giant breaking up his buffet, because suddenly his head popped out from one of the holes in the bag. He looked up at me and froze, no doubt surprised by the vision of my gargantuan head, then he made a hasty retreat and in seconds he was gone. In milliseconds he'd run past the washing products, around the shoe cleaner and down the edge of the shelf unit, and I last saw his tail moving at the speed of light towards the back of the cupboard. It was time to act and sort this out once and for all. I didn't want to be scooping poop day in and day out. I needed to communicate with the mice.

I thought it could be confusing to try and communicate with all of the mice at once, so I requested that just one come forward and talk to me, the one in charge, the head mouse. I began by sending a feeling of love. Within moments I received a picture of a mouse in my mind's eye and I could tell from his body language that he wasn't happy. I tried to begin a conversation with him, but he wasn't listening. He was livid.

'I'd like to talk about the food you're eating,' I said to him quietly.

He screamed at me, furiously waving his furry arms as he spoke. 'I'm not going to stop eating! You don't understand. You humans are all the same – you're bullies. You don't care for us. What am I meant to do? It's cold! I have a family to feed!'

I couldn't get a word in edgeways.

'There's plenty of food. Why not share? Is it asking too much?' he said, punctuating his words with deep intakes of breath. 'You have so much food. I don't have any. I have a family. Why don't you care about my family?'

'But …' I tried to break in, but he continued straight over me.

'We're only eating what we need, and you have so much. *So much food!* We're hungry. We need to eat,' he said, clearly furious.

'Of course,' I interrupted finally. 'I'm happy to share.'

For the first time he stopped screaming at me. He had a confused look on his face and was silent. I didn't hesitate – I took this opportunity to explain.

'I understand you need to feed your family to stay alive. I'm not asking you to stop eating the food. I just want to make a deal with you,' I told him.

Head Mouse looked at me with a quizzical look in his eyes.

'I suggest that during the cold months I leave you and your family some of the dog biscuits in a white dish. The rest of the food is out of bounds. Every day, at the same time as I feed my own animals, I'll leave food out for you.'

He lowered his fists from their position on his hips and let out a sigh.

'When it gets warmer,' I went on, 'I'd like you to leave and find your own food outside. You see, the smell is overwhelming to my human nose. I'd also like you to understand this is a special arrangement just between us. Please don't tell your friends.'

I could just imagine word getting out that food was available on tap at the house with the white front door – it would become a free-for-all for every mouse family in the neighbourhood.

'So, is it a deal? Do you agree to the arrangements?' I said to Head Mouse.

He seemed totally overwhelmed, both moved and relieved. 'Yes!' he said enthusiastically, and I felt two strong arms wrapping around me, giving me a big hug and the most immense feeling of joy and love.

'Promise?' I said.

'Promise,' he replied, smiling, and there it was, cast in stone.

I was relieved to know I'd only be scooping the poop for a limited time and there was an end in sight.

The next morning I kept to my side of the deal and filled my dog's bowl, my cat's bowl and the white dish for the mice. I checked back 30 minutes later and the dish was empty. No sign of a mouse. In the evening, the feeding schedule was repeated.

The routine was always the same and it appeared the mice knew the meal times. I'd put down the dish then check back barely ten minutes later and it would be empty, with never a sign of cute hairless ears or a long tail diving for cover. We'd reached a compromise, existing as one large family under the same roof with twice-daily waitress service. Happy the mice were leaving the bags of food untouched, I continued with the arrangement and the weeks ticked past.

Then one day something changed. I checked and the biscuits were still there. I wondered whether the mice were a little full after weeks of eating. However, at suppertime the dish was still full of biscuits. This time I wondered whether they were ill. For a couple of days I anxiously opened the door, hoping it would be empty, but it was always full. I felt a loss – my little family under the stairs had gone.

It took me a few days to accept the truth. The buds of spring had begun to show their beautiful petals and the daffodils were peeking through the soil. As I'd got stuck into the routine of feeding, I'd forgotten the details of our agreement. Of course, it had grown warmer and the mice had gone. The head mouse had kept to the deal. A promise is a promise.

This experience changed my perspective on mice. I'd had no idea how determined they were and how keen to be understood. Ultimately, I'd had no idea they were so loyal, so emotional and so honest. Head Mouse had opened my eyes to a different side of his species and also proven that … mice don't renege on a promise.

❧ *Morgan's Wake-Up Call* ❧

I continued to invite friends to let me communicate with their animals. I was still working in theatre as a stage manager and fitted the communications around my full-time job. I would work in theatre in the evenings and matinées, and would fit the practice in during my time off during the day or on Sunday. Some weeks I'd have three or four requests and people would have to wait a while and other weeks were quieter and I could help them pretty quickly. The wonderful result of this continued pursuit of accuracy was that my confidence grew. The more communications I practised, the more I learned about my own personal style, pitfalls and obstacles.

Whenever I found time, I sat in silence with Morgan or Texas and asked them about their day. Morgan works with me on a subtle level, more subconsciously, which is how many of us may relate to our animals. He hardly ever talks and when he does it is normally with short, succinct, to the point sentences. He's an earthy kind of dog, with a huge connection to Spirit, or the Source. Not that you'd realize this straight away, because above and beyond these qualities, he's a dog. That's his essence and it would be wrong to treat him as any other living being.

Morgan's passion, like that of most dogs, is food. Walking him in the summer is like going on an obstacle course where the aim is to scoot him around as many picnickers as possible. His mission, on the other hand, is to zig-zag, targeting as many picnics as possible before he's stopped. He often cleverly outmanoeuvres me and doubles back before I've noticed. In his advanced years – he's now about 15 – he's learned that looking sweet and 'starving' has a higher rate of success than being pushy and barging. He trots over to a family having a picnic and sits looking cute. They fall for it and bingo, he's fed another sausage or sandwich. Occasionally his heart rules his manners. He has been known to lick a small child's ice cream as she's strolled by unaware. And any food on the floor is, of course, fair game, including the bread being fed to the ducks – one of his regular treats.

When I'm not available to take Morgan out he has a dog walker. He's hilarious when he comes back from these days out with other dogs. It's like he's been out on the town with the boys. He comes in the front door full of doggie testosterone, bounding down the hall, toenails clattering on the tiles, jumping and leaping around. Texas knows to stay clear when he's like this. It's as if he's all pumped up after a trip to the gym.

After my initial success, I lost my confidence in being able to talk to Morgan and Texas. It felt so much harder with them rather than an animal I didn't know, because I presumed I knew what they would answer back. To overcome this technical hitch I'd pretend we were strangers and kept reminding myself to 'stay in neutral', which meant I couldn't have any agenda or expectation. Slowly, I began to trust myself, and the odd snippet of information became a couple of snippets, then a sentence, then a whole movie clip of images until I'd found a nice flow. I'd ask them how they got on with one another when I wasn't there and whether Morgan liked his dog walker, and pleaded with Texas to stay safe and out of trouble, at which point he'd almost raise his furry eyebrows and sigh.

As our communication progressed, I began to play about with it: I'd ask them a question out loud, instead of silently in my mind, and then I'd wait for the response. Texas particularly liked this game at bedtime. I'd find him lying at the end of the bed, paws curled under his chest, eager-eyed, waiting for me to pop the first question.

Domestic animals who live closely with us are affected by our decisions. I was planning a three-week holiday to Australia and had already gone ahead and arranged for Morgan to stay with his dog walker, who boards dogs in his home. I hadn't told him about the holiday, but he'd tuned into me and worked out I was going to be leaving him behind. When I made the mistake of not considering his feelings, he put me right in a startling way.

We were on his regular morning walk on the common when he suddenly ran into the middle of a very busy road. Thankfully no cars were coming and I was able to catch up with him and put him back on the lead. He waited a day and then the next morning he did it again. This time cars were travelling at about 40 mph right towards him. I ran out into the road and stood in front of them, frantically waving my arms to get them to stop. They saw me in time and I was able to catch Morgan and walk him to the pavement, my legs shaking with the fear that he could have been knocked down. If he'd wanted to put the frighteners on me, he'd achieved it.

When he did the very same thing for a third time, the penny finally dropped. Rather than employing a dog behaviouralist who would have possibly told me to be more of a pack leader, I did what felt right for me. Instead of telling Morgan off with, 'What were you thinking? You know you shouldn't run into the road. You could have got yourself killed!', I did what I should have done the very first time: '*Why* are you running into the road, Morgan?'

'To get your attention,' he replied.

'Well, now you have it. What's the matter?' I said.

'You didn't ask me. What's the point of being able to communicate if you don't listen to us?' he said.

I fell silent, lost for words. Is this what he had nearly killed himself for? He was right, though. What's the point of opening a door if you only shut it again? I needed to acknowledge that this new interaction we had was two-way and mutually beneficial.

'What didn't I ask you? What do you want to say?' I replied.

'You didn't ask me what I wanted,' he stated.

Then it dawned on me – I was packing him off to the dog walker's home and I hadn't even asked him whether he was OK with it. I hadn't involved him in the decision at all. I apologized to him and told him I understood why he was mad. He reminded me we were equals. He gave me a picture of a square, which he divided into four equal parts. Each part was assigned to a member of the family – me, my partner, Texas and Morgan himself. This was how he viewed us – as equals.

Morgan has never got my attention like this again. He hasn't needed to. I now explain when I'm going away and involve him in every decision that affects him.

CHAPTER 3

The Texas Ranger

THIS IS MY introduction to Texas, the green-eyed red-headed feline in my life, and a glimpse into his free spirit. Texas has made it clear to me that just because it's possible to communicate with animals, it doesn't give us the right to control them.

It began when I became aware that Texas was disappearing for long periods at a time. This went on for a number of weeks. I'd call him but he wouldn't appear. This was strange in itself, as he's the most wonderfully responsive cat who rushes to me when I call his name. As he does so he is normally calling, 'I'm here, I'm here,' or sometimes, 'I'm coming, I'm coming,' which I'll hear way off in the distance, and a minute or so later he might appear at the top of my garden fence or on the shed roof.

I was becoming more concerned about his long absences, but talking to your own animals isn't always easy. I thought I could use my new skill to keep tabs on him, but he had other plans.

On one of his absent days I reached out to ask him, 'Where are you?'

He replied, 'On important cat business.'

'What do you mean, "important cat business"? Where are you?' I said.

'None of *your* business,' he replied, completely self-assured.

After that I tried to connect with him on a visual level to look out of his eyes to establish where he was. He blocked the connection. He simply wouldn't let me in.

The extended absences carried on for another week and I continued to try and find out what he was up to, but the answer was always the same: 'I'm on important cat business.' When he returned he wasn't asking for food in his usual demanding way and I became suspicious he was dining elsewhere. The biggest giveaway was the tell-tale scent – he kept coming home smelling of another woman's perfume!

'I know you're moonlighting with another woman,' I said to him. 'I can smell her perfume on you.'

Texas just carried on as though we were talking about the weather. He wasn't fussed.

My suspicions were justified one day when I received a call from a soft-voiced woman. 'Hello, I've just got your number from your cat's tag. He's ginger?' she said.

'Yes, that's him,' I confirmed.

'I've been seeing him around here a lot lately and wondered whether you knew he was here.'

'No, I didn't know,' I said. 'I knew he was going somewhere and I've been trying to find out where it was. Is he with you now?'

'He was a minute ago. I'll just go back outside and have a look.' She disappeared from the phone and a moment later was back. 'He's right outside,' she said.

'I'll come straight over,' I said, and she told me her street and house number.

I raced round to meet her, and wouldn't you know it, there was Texas looking like the cat that had got the cream. I picked him up and then the lady invited me inside to tell me what she'd noticed. She revealed she'd been seeing Texas going in and out of her neighbour's large ground-floor window. As a cat lover with a feline companion of her own, she knew the unwritten rule – you don't feed other people's cats – and she decided to bring this to the attention of her neighbour, who in return became suspiciously non-committal. I thanked her for kindly giving me the heads up and I carried Texas home.

When he went missing the next evening I went straight round to the street and called him. I walked up and down the houses and eventually found him in a garden close to the house with the large window. I carried him home again and fed him. 'Please come home at night,' I said. He smiled, purred and ate his tuna supper.

The next evening it happened again and I went calling for him as loudly as is possible at 11 o'clock at night without waking up the whole street. He wasn't homeless, he wasn't a stray, I wasn't on holiday. In fact, he was the most loved cat on the planet – in my opinion – albeit an unashamedly passionate food hunter, preferring the easy to catch version that came in a dish.

My cries must have been heard, as the window remained shut for the following few days and Texas fell back into his normal routine and was now home at night.

This led me to understand that we're only in the position of guardians to animals. We don't own them and it's certainly not a good idea to expect them to do things against their will. We can only communicate with them as far as they will let us. They will always have their own agenda and their own free will.

This wasn't the first time Texas had gone on an adventure. In fact, moonlighting was in his blood. Ever since he'd run out of his cage at Battersea Dogs' Home and pressed his stunning golden fur against my legs, I'd been charmed. But I wasn't the only one. He's continued to charm women ever since, and now he's nine, so that's quite a bit of charming.

The first to join his harem were two young career women who lived in the ground-floor flat two doors down. Texas soon worked out they had fallen for him and he came up with an idea that would make his life easier. He would sit on the window ledge at the front of their flat and call out to them. Within moments the front door would open and he'd jump down and walk inside, bold and fearless. He'd walk down their hallway until he reached their back door. Standing still, he'd give another command to open the back door, and when it was open he'd walk straight out. All he had to do now was shimmy through to the next garden and climb up the rear fire escape and he'd be in his cat flap. That short cut saved him at least 10 minutes of 'pointless' effort going all the way down the street, avoiding dogs, feet and cars, cutting through the busy alley and finally making his way carefully across other cats' gardens until he eventually reached mine. Soon he got wise that it could work the other way too. He'd call out at their back door, walk down the hall and then wait for them to open the front door. He had them twisted round his ivory-white whiskers.

It was quite a long time before one of the girls admitted what Texas was up to. He'd kept his little secret for at least six months. I was told he'd occasionally divert from his usual plan and go into one of their bedrooms to lie on their bed, where, of course, he'd receive much love and admiration. This was the first time he came home smelling of another woman's perfume; he was only 12 months old.

I liked and trusted these women and thought Texas's short cut was a stroke of genius, so I laughed along with them and Texas continued to use their home as his short cut and rest stop for the next three years until we moved from the area.

At a different time I saw another example of Texas' free will. I was standing in the kitchen of my first-floor flat, hands in the washing-up bowl, looking out of the window to the first-floor flat opposite, when I had to look twice. I couldn't believe my eyes. There was Texas curled up asleep on the bed. It was summer and their back door was open, so he'd just wandered up their fire escape and found himself somewhere soft to sleep. I banged on the window, calling his name. He looked up from his pillow and chose to ignore me.

It appeared he felt he owned all the flats around us, because another time I saw him on the sofa of the downstairs flat.

They'd left one of their windows open. There now numbered four flats in his portfolio.

So what I've learned over the years is that Texas is a free spirit. Animals are masters in their own right and you can't keep tabs on them just because you can talk to them. It's not possible to control them or tell them what to do. Texas is his own cat and he makes no apology for that. It's one of the qualities I absolutely love about him.

I have also come to terms with the necessity to swallow my pride and admit I'm not the only woman in his life, although I console myself knowing our hearts are as one. He also now adores Jennie, who comes and looks after him when I'm away. He's always waiting for her on the doorstep as her car pulls up, whatever time of day it is, and he curls up on her lap while she watches TV. He liked the little old lady down the road when she was buying in cat food especially for him, even though it had been a long time since she'd lived with a cat. He loved the two career women in the ground-floor flat who understood their hallway was also his right of way and they were his gatekeepers. And he loved having more than one soft place to rest his weary ginger head.

What I've also realized is that cats are clever and able to manipulate things to their own advantage. For example, instead of using animal communication to do something I wanted, Texas soon used it to get me to do something *he* wanted. It was the middle of the night when it happened and I was sound asleep. Then I woke, bolt upright. I had heard Texas call out to me in my dream. I have hearing that's finely tuned to his tone of meow, just as a mother can distinguish between the cries of her child and other children. Then I received an image in my mind and I knew he was at the front door. Like a zombie, still half asleep, I immediately knew what he wanted and stumbled down the stairs. I unlocked the door and pulled it open. In trotted Texas, a little late for his mutually agreed curfew. 'Purrutt,' he said in thanks, as he pushed himself into my legs.

When I communicate with cats I know I have to be extra careful, because they often only say what they want you to hear. They sometimes withhold the truth altogether, whereas I find dogs are much more honest and generally say it how it is. They are much more reliable that way.

Texas hasn't stopped courting women, of any age. The three-year-old Spanish girl next door is absolutely crazy about him. She always stops, points to him through the eye-level gap in my front gate and tells her mother, 'Meow meow, meow meow,' as her face lights up and she grins from ear to ear. Texas sits soaking up the admiration – he adores his fans.

CHAPTER 4

Finding Conviction

WHAT IF YOU begin to receive information directly from an animal? Maybe you suddenly start to hear your own animals at home. Or you receive a wave of emotional joy when you casually ask your friend's cat what kind of day she's having. What do you do?

In the books I'd gathered round me like a comforting blanket, I kept reading the word 'psychic', and while this had never been mentioned as the method of animal communication in the workshops I'd attended, it was obviously very relevant. I needed to know what 'being psychic' and 'psychic communication' involved, and in my search I came across the College of Psychic Studies, so I signed up for the Foundation Programme.

The College of Psychic Studies is located in the trendy and expensive borough of Chelsea and Kensington. It is hidden within a cleverly disguised four-storey Georgian building set within a long terrace of private homes, only a couple of gigantic Tyrannosaurus strides away from the Natural History

Museum. It was originally founded in 1884 by a small group of people, including some notable scientists and dignitaries of the clergy, who were there primarily to investigate psychic and mediumistic phenomena, a popular subject even back in the Victorian era.

One of the early founders was Sir Arthur Conan Doyle, a physician who became renowned for his Sherlock Holmes series. In the late 1800s, Sir Arthur joined the Society for Psychical Research (SPR) and carried out experiments with a woman called Mrs Ball. Evidence from these experiments convinced him that telepathy was genuine and he dedicated the next 30 years to further studies and investigations and wrote 14 books on psychic matters, including his most substantial one, *The History of Spiritualism*.

When I looked at the college brochure, I was drawn to one particular class called 'Psychic Unfoldment', led by Avril Price. I'd never heard of her before, but I liked her down-to-earth humour when we spoke over the phone and her class sounded interesting because it covered a huge range of psychic skills, including psychometry, reading auras and mediumship.

I was feeling apprehensive as I walked from the crisp spring air through the dark blue main door and into the building. I tried to look relaxed as I waited for the receptionist to point me in the right direction. Behind me on the walls were large gold-framed oil paintings with the names of respected psychic scholars, scientists and clergy dating back over the last century. I liked the fact that I was walking amongst history – it somehow felt more authentic.

Up until this point I had thought all psychics were like Mystic Meg – gypsy types with a crystal ball – and I felt distrustful of this age-worn image. Even now when I receive small flyers through my letterbox from psychics advertising they can resolve my emotional life or eliminate past-life karma, I throw them straight into the recycling bin.

So when I met Avril, my psychic teacher, I was gobsmacked. Gone was the kooky, mystical fortune-teller with long curling fingernails, gold hoop earrings and crystal ball in tow, and in stepped the Jo Brand equivalent. She was normal and she had that dry, satirical sense of humour on which the English co-medienne has made her reputation. I thought she was fabulous!

Over the next eight weeks she led me through the unfold-ing of my own psychic ability. Crikey! In the beginning I didn't even know what being 'grounded' meant. Though it was a term I'd often heard used at the animal communication workshops, I still thought it was something that would happen to me if I were discovered doing something naughty, just like at school. I felt lucky to have been drawn to Avril from the many teach-ers at the college. I could connect with her down-to-earth non-threatening approach and the way she made psychic development both fun and accessible. In a world that could be considered scary or fairy-like, I had found someone who was neither.

After this first class Avril let me move straight up to the next level, Psychic Development at Intermediate/Advanced Level. During this second term I wanted to push myself, to go beyond my comfort zone. It was a place of learning after all, so there was no better place to try something new. I signed up for the Platform in Mediumship, where I'd be expected to bring concrete evidence and comfort through from those in the spirit world.

One evening, in front of 150 students and friends of the college packed to the walls, I stood on the platform at the front and prayed the spirit of someone would come through to give me a message to pass on to someone in the audience. I was quietly hoping an animal would come through, but in fact it was a man who contacted me from the Other Side with a message for his grandson. All through the delivery of the message, my legs were quaking. I was certain everyone could see how nervous and scared I felt. Despite this, the message was clear and the grandson understood it and was grateful to hear from his grandfather. I can now admit this was one of the most nerve-wracking experiences of my life, but it did help me enormously. I feel the only way we can gain confidence is by pushing ourselves further than is comfortable. In this way we can grow.

At about the same time I also trained in Reiki, the energy system created by Mikao Usui for self-healing, self-development and spiritual development. I began with Reiki level 1. I was hungry for what Reiki was giving me: deep relaxation and a sense of bliss. About three months later, I trained to practitioner level 2. I found making this connection with energy was a good foundation for subtler energy work with animals. It also made me more receptive as a conduit for energy and I developed more sensitivity in my hands. Reiki attunements restore connections to higher energies, the Source, God – call it whichever is most comfortable for you. Personally, I find the word 'God' tricky, as I had a completely non-religious upbringing and still consider myself non-religious, but I do now believe in a higher source or divine energy which we can all draw on for answers and support.

I definitely feel Reiki has enhanced my work and it has also taught me the importance of breath and of intention. Breath can help increase healing and, as the saying goes, 'Where intention goes, energy flows.' As an animal communicator I now work with the breath and my intention – using my breath to calm my nervous system and relax my body, and my intention to remain neutral and work for the highest good of the animal.

After several months of spiritual development, in the summer I felt drawn to attend another animal communication workshop.

🐾 *The Animals' Ambassador* 🐾

The first time I saw Amelia Kinkade she was gliding past me in a long, sparkling, deep purple cloak and high heels. She was as American as a lady from Los Angeles could be; she had *that look*: slim, toned, tanned and highly polished, with cascading curly blonde hair. She was beautiful.

At that time Amelia was a professional animal communicator with over a decade's experience. She was teaching all over the world and had her first book in the shops, *Straight from the Horse's Mouth*. It was the best book on animal communication I'd ever read – and I'd read a few. The stories were incredible, hilarious and deeply moving. After I'd read it and discovered Amelia was coming to teach in England, I had another intuitive feeling – I knew I wanted to meet her. That is how in the summer of 2005 I came to be sitting in the dining room of 'Brightlife', a beautiful Georgian mansion dedicated to enlightenment and rejuvenation, on the TT motor-cycle-racing Isle of Man.

On a Friday evening, two dozen or so people were sitting inside a function room with a wall of windows overlooking a field full of munching sheep. Amelia introduced the theory behind animal communication and its connection with science and quantum physics. She began by telling us that everything is energy. Human beings are energy, plants are energy and animals are energy. All this energy is connected on the most gargantuan spider's web, a 3D picture which spreads out in every direction throughout the universe. Amelia called this 'the Zero Point Energy Field'. She went on to elaborate that quantum physicists now tell us that every living being and physical object has a resonant holographic image logged on to the spider's web (Zero Point Energy Field). This image is called a quantum hologram. This theory means you have a hologram, I have a hologram and so do our animals. All of us are connected, because our holograms are attached on the web, despite the fact that you are sitting there and I am sitting here.

As Amelia spoke about the harmony of science and psychic connection, it dawned on me that she was in a completely different league from the other teachers I'd met. Her understanding of animal communication was immense. When I witnessed her own ability to talk to animals and her deep heartfelt love of them, it gave me cause to feel inspired. I could see just how far you could take this ability and I knew I had a lot of work ahead of me. Amelia was setting the standard for animal communicators everywhere. She was then, and would remain, a huge source of inspiration to me, as well as hundreds of other devoted animal lovers across the globe, a role model for professional animal communicators and an ambassador for animals.

After the in-depth and brain-expanding explanation of animal communication, we were invited to try our first communication with a little white and tan terrier. His guardian had brought him in for us to communicate with and he stayed for the next 40 minutes. This was the first workshop I'd attended where a 'real live animal' came to help us practice – an animal guest-teacher.

The first question Amelia wanted us to ask him was: 'What's his favourite food?' She told us to imagine sending an empty food bowl to him using a picture in our mind's eye and asking him to fill it with his favourite food then return it to us.

By this time I had already attended four animal communication workshops, I knew how to make a connection with an animal and how to ask questions. This should have been puppy-play for me. However, all I felt was blank. It was as if an empty void had washed over me. I couldn't connect. I couldn't receive the answers. But the most disastrous feeling of all was the *nothingness*. I desperately tried to feel an emotional connection with the cute little dog who had taken a liking to my trousers and had begun licking them in earnest. Despite his joyful distraction, I felt numb. My heart felt closed.

After a couple of minutes' silence, Amelia asked, 'What did you get?'

'Nothing,' I replied.

She continued around the room hearing what everyone else had either seen or heard.

The second question was: 'What about his favourite activity?'

'What have you got?' she cajoled.

'Nothing,' I said despondently.

'Nothing at all?'

'No, nothing.' I found myself shrinking into my chair as everyone's eyes fell upon me.

'Can you see what his bed is like?' Amelia encouraged.

'No,' I replied uncomfortably. I felt worse and worse. With each question I felt another nail being driven into my complete lack of ability. I had lost it. The special connection had gone.

Amelia looked at me, confused, 'Did you receive anything?' It was as though she could tell something wasn't quite right and that this was new for me.

'Nothing, nothing at all.'

I wanted to run – run away from the knowledge that I couldn't communicate with animals anymore. The wonderful ability I had discovered just six months earlier had vanished for good.

Back at my guesthouse, I fell into a deep dark despair. I went to bed feeling as though I couldn't speak about this to any of the other students and ended up tossing and turning all night.

The next day I tried to start afresh and entered the workshop room with positive thoughts. But when we began to practice our communication skills again, I struggled whilst most of the people around me seemed to find it effortless. They appeared to communicate with dogs and cats as if they'd been doing it all their life. But for me, it was another disappointing day.

Over supper that evening I had the good fortune to sit next to a talented animal communicator called Yvette Knight. She had been having amazingly accurate communications all day.

'How are you doing?' she asked me.

'Not good,' I admitted.

'Oh, really? Why's that?' she asked, genuinely interested.

'I just can't feel anything – anything at all.'

I went on to tell her of an animal communication workshop earlier in the year, where I'd chosen to believe someone else rather than trust my own inner voice. Understandably, this had the result of completely undermining my confidence in my ability as an effective animal communicator.

'I feel as though my heart has shut down,' I told her.

Now Yvette is a belly dancer of gladiator proportions, with long blonde hair and the wit to disarm even the smartest of opponents. Shy and retiring, she is not. So she was very empathetic and for a while simply listened, which was just what I needed – then she came out with a few hand-picked expletives and I felt a bit better for sharing my feelings.

🐾 *Jupiter's Magic* 🐾

Sunday morning arrived, along with the last two sessions before my flight back to London. Yvette was having breakfast at a private table with Amelia, so I joined some women on the grand dining table and earwigged an interesting conversation about shamanism. It seemed that the basic principle of shamanism was the belief that everything is alive and has a spirit, and shamans try to live in harmony with the Earth and animals.

An hour later, the students and I were sitting in an oval-shaped pattern around the edge of the lecture room anticipating Amelia's arrival. She walked in as though she meant business and launched into the importance of staying centred and grounded within your own power. She wasn't talking about a masculine, dominating, controlling power, but that internal power all of us have as part of our individual birthright, the power that keeps us strong and protected. As she spoke, it felt as though everyone else disappeared and the room descended into silence until all I heard were her words.

Although she didn't look my way, I felt she had crafted her speech just for me. She spoke at length and then ended with a short summary.

'Don't ever give your power away,' she said. 'You must keep it close, because there are those who will try to take it from you. Don't let them.'

Easier said than done, I thought, but it immediately struck a chord, and I remembered my feelings of emptiness when someone had implied I should not trust my own intuition, my own gut feelings.

The air was cool, but the sun was shining upon us as we walked outside with our notepads and pens to meet our first animal guest teacher of the morning. In the centre of the courtyard stood a tall dark horse called Jupiter. He appeared very calm and very proud. After a disastrous day and a half, I didn't have high hopes, but I tried to communicate with him anyway.

Within seconds of looking into Jupiter's deep chocolate eyes, my chest started to rise and fall as my breathing became deeper and more demanding. I began to feel an overwhelming rush of love from him that seemed to cloak my entire body. My legs were shaking, overcome by this sudden surge of emotion. Worried that I was about to make a right fool of myself in front of everyone, I made a hasty retreat from the group to the side of the building behind us. Tears were pouring down my face as I tried to compose myself, struggling to control my breathing and desperately trying not to sob out loud in front of this group of relative strangers.

Whenever I looked at Jupiter to ask him one of the questions from Amelia, I felt another wave of love washing over me, soaking into every pore of my skin and reaching deep inside my heart. His love was so strong it might be compared to the love that pours out of your heart when welcoming your first newborn into the world or to the power of Niagara Falls. His love was instinctual, all-encompassing and utterly powerful. Jupiter was blasting my heart wide open and enabling me to connect with my emotions.

At that moment, I vowed never to give my power away again. I will always be hugely grateful to this magnificent horse who managed to see straight through to the core of me. He tuned into me, even when I was unable to tune into him, and he helped me in the exact way I needed, by opening my heart connection. Later I'd learn that this could also be called heart chakra healing. Horses seem to have an extraordinary talent in this arena.

After this immensely healing experience with Jupiter, my communications with animals went from strength to strength. I could sense an emotional connection with them, whether they were sad, happy, grieving, joyful or confused. With my heart reawakened, I could understand any emotion they were feeling and this enabled me to connect with them on a deeper level. It helped me on a personal level, too, because now I was able to ascertain whether I was truly connected to an animal or just making it up.

As I left the island I felt more experienced, inspired and whole again. In just one weekend, Amelia and Jupiter had managed to put me right back on track.

It wasn't until I was flying through the clouds over the Irish Sea that I remembered that my zodiac sign's ruling planet happens to be Jupiter, and I wondered whether this was merely coincidence or a strange twist of fate. As someone born under the sign of Sagittarius, my zodiac symbol is a hybrid of half human above and half horse below – maybe this *was* a sign of synchronicity.

Opening the Door of Opportunity

VERY EARLY ON in my animal communication experience I was drawn to two dogs, Mono and Riki. I discovered both of these animals in January 2006, when there were pleas on their behalf on separate web forums where I had membership. Each time an impulse made me want to contact their guardians to volunteer my services as an animal communicator. It turned out eventually that I wasn't solely helping the dogs, they were also helping me, as if fate, or the universe, had brought us together for a reason. They taught me a lot about ill-health and positive attitude and were instrumental in building my confidence as an effective animal communicator. More on Riki later, but first let me tell you about Mono.

🐾 *Mono, Mike and Moe* 🐾

I came across Mono when I received an e-mail from a friend who gave me a link to his story. When I clicked on the link, there was a piece on Mono saying he'd had an accident which had paralysed him from the neck down and there was the possibility he might never walk again. There was a photo of him with an appeal asking for help of any kind. It showed a collie-like dog with soft shining eyes and I felt my heart pounding in my chest. When I gazed at him, I immediately knew I wanted to contact his guardian to see if he was open to my work as an animal communicator. It was still the early days of my journey into animal communication and I was working two jobs – my full-time job in theatre and my part-time job as an animal communicator – but a part of me knew I had to find the time to offer my help.

And so one Saturday night I nervously rang Mike to offer my services without payment. I introduced myself and talked about my work as an animal communicator and how I thought I might be able to help.

Of course this call came out of the blue for him. 'To be honest, I don't know quite what to make of this,' he said, in an open-minded and down-to-earth way. 'I've never even heard of animal communication.'

'I can act like a telephone line between you and Mono,' I explained, 'which would give Mono the means to tell you what he's feeling.'

I don't think Mike really understood what I was offering, not in its entirety, but he was willing to give it a try.

'I'd really like to know if he can tell you what happened,' he said. 'I was out walking and threw a stick and then heard him yelp in pain. When I caught up with him he was lying on his side, unable to move his legs.' Mike spoke with a huge amount of warmth in a slightly gruff kind of way; there was no disguising what he felt for Mono.

'I'll have a go and if I can connect with him we can ask him that question,' I replied. 'Would you mind giving me a call back in about an hour?'

Mike agreed and rang me back as arranged.

'Were you able to connect with him?' he asked in a tone that was both apprehensive and sceptical.

'Yes, I think so, but let's find out. I'm going to start by going through a few pieces of information with you, which I'd like you to verify. All you have to do is say whether they make sense to you or not. You can just say "yes" or "no" if you like.'

'All right,' he said.

'Mono gave me the colour blue and then pictured himself lying across a sofa with you lying below him on the floor. Right at this moment, while we're speaking, he shows himself lying on his left side on the sofa.'

'Mono is lying on his left side, just as you say, and yes, he's on the sofa,' Mike said, almost incredulously. 'He's in the lounge and the walls are blue. I felt he'd be more comfortable here. I'm sleeping on the floor close to him so I can check on him and because I'm too nervous to sleep far away. Besides, he can't move by himself, so I have to turn him regularly to prevent pressure sores.'

'The next picture he gave me was of a woman with frown lines. He wants to tell the lady not to worry.'

'That will be my partner, Moe. She's always speaking about her frown lines.'

'Can you let her know that Mono tells her not to worry?' Mike said he would. 'When I communicated with Mono,' I went on, 'he drew my attention to his neck and said there was something on the back of it that was bothering him. He said he didn't know what it was, but I sensed it was irritating him.'

'He has a slow-release morphine patch stapled to his neck,' Mike told me a little quietly. 'It gives him three days' slow relief.'

'He's also describing his back legs feeling weak and I can feel his front legs are like jelly and he's exhausted.'

'Can he tell us what happened?' said Mike. There was a sense of keenness in his voice now.

'Mono showed me a movie clip of himself tripping over a small hole in the ground, like an uneven surface that caught him unawares. He's giving me the impression he was running, put his foot in a hole, went flying and twisted, then landed heavily,' I answered him.

Mike said, 'It had got dark, but Mono was insisting on one more throw of the stick and I gave in. He chased after it, disappearing out of sight. From the gloom I heard a deep whine, then it went silent. That's when I came across him lying flat on his side, motionless. I thought he might have broken one of his legs. I lifted him up to carry him to the car and his legs just dangled. We took him straight to his vet.'

With Mono's version of the same event, Mike now had a fuller picture. I continued to relay what I'd received from Mono.

'He tells me he's receiving healing,' I said.

'Yes,' said Mike.

'He wants you to know he is happy with it, but he can heal himself given time.'

'He can?' said Mike, slightly breathless.

'That's what he told me. He also says the healing is helping make the recovery process faster and he'd like some more please. He'd like you to give him some healing too.'

'Our friend, Liz Darcy, is coming round every day,' Mike explained. 'She's a reflexologist as well as a healer and she's been giving him Reiki. In fact it was Liz who decided to put Mono's picture on the website. She's the one who broadcast the appeal.'

'It's great he's receiving healing from Liz,' I replied, 'and I can send him some too. He wants to thank you for doing what he calls "the undignified things" with such sensitivity.'

There was a short pause before Mike spoke again. 'He needs 24-hour care and he also needs catheterizing every morning. It might not be pleasant for me, but I'd do anything for him. I'm more concerned that it's not very dignified for him, so I try to do it as quickly as possible and without any fuss. I think he prefers it that way.'

It was clear to me that Mike adored Mono, not only by his actions but also by the warmth in his voice, and Mono wanted to share his feelings in return.

'Mono says he loves you so much,' I told Mike, 'and I feel a huge love when he thinks of you and when he answers your questions. He absolutely adores you.'

There was such a sense of gentleness, admiration and togetherness between Mono and Mike, it was as if they had an invisible cord connecting their hearts.

I now delivered Mono's final message: 'Mono wants to tell you, "I will be the dog I used to be."'

'He said that?' said Mike. '"I will be the dog I used to be?"'

'Yes.'

There was a moment's silence then Mike said, 'Since Mono's birth in 1997, we've climbed the mountains of Snowdonia together, with me pushing him up rock gullies. Sometimes he'd reach the top before me and look down as if to say, "Where've you been?" In winter we've plodded through snowdrifts as deep as he is. Oh, for sure, he's had his moments – the odd night in police kennels, even four nights in a dogs' home. Each time he's gone missing, it's probably because he's been running after a sheep or a rabbit. The late 1990s were dark times for me because I was splitting up with my ex-partner, but Mono kept me sane. I'm a nomadic fishing historian and he has been able to go everywhere with me, including to kipper shows, where he's become known as the "kipper-dog". His long bushy tail has also earned him the nickname of "Basil Brush". He's travelled all over Britain in my campervan and when he got his own pet passport he came with me to my house 3,000 feet up in the Greek mountains. He even found love with a Greek girlfriend called Zina. He's not just a part of the family, he's the central figure in it, and my soul mate. What kind of man would I be if I turned my back on my best friend now?'

I began to admire this man who wouldn't give up on his dog. Some might have said things were as bad as they could be and the kindest thing would be to put Mono to sleep. After all, he appeared paralysed from the neck down. But Mike wouldn't turn his back on his friend, especially once he'd received the knowledge that Mono himself could see a bright future.

'I felt nervous calling you back,' he admitted. 'I wasn't sure whether I was clutching at straws or whether I really believed you. You'd sounded entirely genuine when you called me, but a doubt still lingered. Still, as you began recounting to me what you'd learned from Mono, I was flabbergasted. There were things you simply couldn't have known.'

From that moment on Mike decided that nothing was going to stop him helping Mono back onto his feet. Each day he and Moe would support Mono using towels like hammocks looped underneath his shoulders and hips to assist his walking, which greatly helped strengthen his muscles.

A couple of weeks later he e-mailed, asking me to communicate with Mono again:

I remember Mono's words as clearly as yesterday: 'I will be the dog I used to be.' The words of that first communication have been widely drawn upon, giving us so much hope and strength to continue, whereas before there were moments when I was questioning whether what we were doing was good for Mono or just us. You've helped us decide on the former.

The second time round I found Mono in greater spirits.

'Everything is helping, especially the love,' he said. 'Love conquers everything.'

'How are you feeling physically?' I said.

'My back legs are still very wobbly, but I'm coping much better. Acupuncture makes me relaxed but sleepy.'

From his sofa position he requested specific music: the theme tune to *Inspector Morse* and Enya's *Orinoco Flow (Sail Away)*.

'I'd also like some fresh air and an interesting view,' he added. It appeared that he was tired of the TV.

'OK, I'll pass on your requests,' I said to him.

Mike went out and bought Mono's music requests and later declared he had become hooked on *Inspector Morse* to the point where he had possibly become the no.1 fan. Hearing that Mono craved a little extra stimulation, he also began to carry him out of the lounge, at first to the door of the conservatory, then later, when the weather was warmer, onto the grass. I felt this extra stimulation would play a large part in Mono's healing.

From then on Mike sent weekly e-mails updating me on Mono's progress. With the healing, the daily visits from Liz, the huge effort on Mono's part, plus that of his guardians and a bottomless pit of love, he began to recover. Within a short span of time I received wonderful news.

'Mono is up on his feet and supporting himself, albeit a bit wobbly,' Mike wrote. 'It's only taken six weeks. Six weeks!'

Then, after about ten weeks, he began to walk – erratically at first, but walk nevertheless. After three months he began to run – after squirrels!

Mono's rate of recovery increased – as did his notoriety. In one e-mail Mike told me their vet, Nicky, had made him her star patient in the practice newsletter, likening him to Rambo! At five months he went back on the road with Mike to the various shows he had to attend.

About nine months after Mono's painful accident I received a message which would blow all other messages out of the water: 'He's climbed a 2,000-foot mountain!'

Despite his initial apprehension, Mike saw the first communication as the turning-point. 'I hung onto those words through the whole process of bringing him back to anywhere near normality. With that impetus we succeeded and without it I'm not sure whether we would have done. In hindsight I can look back on Mono's recovery and see a journey of love.'

Hearing directly from Mono had made a huge difference to how Mike saw him. The communication helped show him that in spite of Mono's fragile physical appearance he had a strength and spirit that wanted to fight. Mono expressed a sheer determination and belief that, with Mike and Moe's love, his recovery would be absolute.

Mike e-mailed:

Today, as I write, I can see Mono lying on the grass outside in the morning sunshine, happy and alert, his eyes as contented as always. He's been Ana [Mike's daughter]'s guardian ever since she was born and is in the process of repeating this with Otis, our newborn. Last Christmas he had a setback in that he got a hefty kick from a horse, but, though it made him wobbly for a couple of weeks, that hasn't stopped him. At the age now of 12, he's still chasing those sticks – in fact he's even chasing trains these days – and loves the sea as much as he ever did. In fact he is in every way, as he said he would be, very much the dog he used to be! In some respects, seeing what he has had to cope with and the way that he did it, he is *more* than the dog he used to be. And he'll always remain my lovely peppercorn-eyed Mono-dog.

Three years after his mountain ascent I had the joy and privilege of meeting Mono face to hairy face. I was teaching a beginners workshop in a manor house near Bath and I'd arranged with Mike for Mono to be a guest teacher.

In the tea break I walked out of the front door and saw a large white van. A tall middle-aged man with curly hair and a friendly weather-worn face climbed out. He looked just as I'd pictured him.

'Hello, Mike,' I greeted him, shaking hands, 'thank you so much for coming. So where is he?'

Mike slid the side door open and there stood a handsome dog with gentle loving eyes.

'Hello, Mono, you gorgeous boy,' I said to him.

Mono jumped down and pushed his body into mine.

'He's not normally this calm,' Mike said. 'It was as though he knew he was coming to see you.'

Then I was able to satisfy one of my heart's desires: I ran my hands through Mono's long black hair and kissed the top of his soft head. My heart leapt into my mouth and I found myself fighting back tears. It felt so moving to be able to touch him, knowing what had happened and what it had taken for him to be standing there. Standing! Pressing his warm body into my legs and looking up with shining, loving eyes at my face. He'd been through so much – he'd suffered acute pain, he'd been disabled and unable to walk, he'd tolerated the indignity of toiletry care and courageously battled on until he found the use of his legs again. Not willing to stop there, with the love of his soul mate Mike, he had gained strength and flexibility and overcome every obstacle placed in front of him. My tears were tears of admiration, relief and ultimately happiness. And Mono had also achieved what many of us only dream of – he'd come back from the brink and climbed a 2,000-foot mountain.

CHAPTER 6

Synchronicity Calls Again

ANIMAL COMMUNICATION workshops are food for the soul. Every time I've attended one I've walked away feeling uplifted, on the biggest high, exhilarated and buzzing.

The first workshop I attended felt like dynamite blasting apart an old belief system that no longer served the truth. At the second workshop I realized I wanted to be an animal communicator. Each workshop I've attended since has been a building block of bringing that dream to fruition.

When I attended my first workshop with Amelia back in 2005 I left full of happiness but also very emotional. By coincidence we shared the same flight back to London and at Heathrow, as we waited for our baggage, I was still overcome by the weekend's experience. The workshop had released something in me and my emotions were bubbling up and over.

'Thank you, thank you for your workshop … Thank you for teaching … You've opened something inside me,' I spluttered, while tears poured down my face. I couldn't say much, but Amelia got the picture.

'Thank *you*,' she said, giving me a hug. No doubt she'd seen this umpteen times before.

I felt raw, and like a newborn baby, I was crying my heart out. It was as though many of the barriers in my life had been removed and the slate had been wiped clean. Since then I have been witness to many people reacting the same way. I have come to learn that animal communication workshops are an emotional business; they have a way of releasing and igniting all in the same breath.

A year later synchronicity would call again, tickling me with her whiskers and giving me a gentle nudge towards Glasgow to attend another of Amelia's workshops. In that time I had completed a stable full of case studies and through experience improved my accuracy. I had also made a decision and had the courage to jump – after a full year of practice, personal development and courses at the psychic college, I had turned professional and was working full-time as an animal communicator.

I was struggling to pay my mortgage in the early months of my new career, but Lady Luck was walking by my side in the weeks leading up to Amelia's workshop. I had known about it for a while and even though I hadn't been able to stop thinking about it, my mind had chosen a different road: 'I can't go, I can't afford it.' Then a friend of mine had booked and I had found my own foot firmly up my backside, giving me the final push. *What are you doing? You have to be there!* shouted my inner voice. I was overwhelmed by the feeling I had to be part of the workshop. But why? My inner voice said, *You're able to help someone there.* That was when my heart took control of the steering wheel and pulled me off the drudge of the grey motorway and onto the colourful winding country roads. I committed to going to the workshop. I didn't know how I was going to afford it, but that hadn't stopped me before.

Literally 30 seconds after I had made up my mind, the phone rang. It was the production manager of the Royal Court Theatre offering me a job.

'Harold Pinter is doing a one-man play called *Krapp's Last Tape* and we'd like you to be the stage manager on it. You've worked with him before and we'd really like you to do it.'

What a gift! Not only did I really want to do the play with Harold, whom I had grown fond of as I had worked alongside him over the previous five years, but it also gave me the vital income I needed to attend the workshop. I wasn't going to come out of theatrical retirement for just anybody, but when Harold Pinter knocks on your door, you open it. There was one small flaw: the dates clashed.

I took a risk and explained to my production manager that I'd love to do it but on one condition: 'I need time off during the first week of rehearsals.' By now my colleagues at the Royal Court knew I was communicating with animals and, being mostly open-minded people, very few of them judged or doubted this huge change of career. The play's director, Ian Rickson, who was also the Royal Court's artistic director at that time, agreed I could take the time off. Here was a good lesson: I had asked for what I wanted and I had received it. Maybe the universe was looking after me, after all. To make sure I wasn't away for too long, I booked an incredibly expensive ticket and ran to catch the train to Scotland.

The night before the workshop I was nervous with anticipation, wondering what I was going to face and excited about seeing Amelia again. In our twin room at the Holiday Express, my friend and I giggled like schoolgirls.

It was a bright morning as I walked into the function room with 30 or so chairs positioned in rows around the edge of a highly polished dance floor. Even though this was a hotel function room, it was a pleasant setting overlooking a sparkling waterfall. I settled myself into a chair next to my friend at the back.

Amelia entered, as stunning as ever, dressed in pink and gold silk. Once she'd settled in and welcomed everyone, she picked me out of the crowd.

'Pea, I see you there. I've been hearing great things about you,' she said.

I puffed up my fur and gave her my best Cheshire-cat smile.

'I hear you've turned professional,' she said with a smile.

'Yes, that's right,' I beamed.

🐾 'Lily Loves You' 🐾

In the morning tea break, I was called over to help a lady who was lying down at the back of the room. Even though she was flat out on the floor next to the bar, she didn't look as though she'd been enjoying too many drinks. As I approached her, I could see tears pouring down her face. Animal communication workshops have a way of helping us get in touch with our inner feelings. They are like glow-worms softly lighting the way deep within our pitch-black cave, guiding us out of the darkness and back into the light. It's an emotional process – there's always a box of tissues at hand. But this was a physical process too.

'It's my back. It does this sometimes. It's so painful I can't move,' the woman gasped.

As I knelt down beside her, I took her hand in mine. I smiled and began talking softly to her. Her name was Judy. I'd been practising Reiki for a number of years by then and this was the reason I'd been picked to go to her. Although I remembered that emotional pain often comes out in physical forms as a way to grab our attention, I didn't channel any Reiki energy that day. I chose to listen to Judy instead and that was when I noticed the shadow of a cat up by her right shoulder. Then I felt overwhelming pangs of loss inside my own chest and the big eyes of the cat boring into me.

'Ask her about it,' the cat gently coaxed me. I wasn't expecting this.

'Why does your back do this?' I said to Judy. 'What are you really feeling? Why do I feel there has been a loss?'

Judy broke down in loud heavy sobs as her heart opened and she began to tell me about the greatest loss of her life: her cat. She had wrapped herself up in chains of guilt, feeling she had let her down.

I glanced across to the cat, who was now sitting proudly by Judy's shoulder, almost smiling. 'Is your cat a startlingly beautiful silver tabby? Does she have a sweet, loving, rather skittish personality with a strong spirit?'

Judy looked straight into my eyes. 'Yes,' she gasped in between sobs. 'She is. She does. She's called … Lily.'

I saw Lily move her glance from Judy back to me and then she gave me her next instruction. I passed the message on: 'Lily has told me she is fine and there is nothing to feel guilty about. I feel she is with you right now.'

'Tell her I never left her,' prompted Lily.

I relayed the message and Judy smiled for the first time. I could see she was hoping it was true but found it hard to comprehend.

Lily continued with her messages.

'She says she is feeling fine and you're not to feel guilty anymore,' I repeated. 'She doesn't blame you for anything. She loves you.'

Judy shared how she felt about Lily until she began to laugh and smile again. As she began to relax, her back began to relax too and she was able to stand and slowly walk outside into the fresh air. She couldn't attend the rest of the workshop because she felt too raw, but spoke about learning animal communication at another time.

When I asked her if I could include her personal experience in this book, she agreed and wrote to share her side of the story:

When my cat Lily fell ill, no one was able to figure out what was wrong with her. Whilst several vets thought it was nothing serious, for months my intuition told me otherwise. I took her to a healer, who said she felt Lily was trying to hide something. The last two weeks of her life were full of pain, confusion and highly intrusive medical procedures. She was finally diagnosed by the veterinary hospital with a nasal tumour, blindness and cancer. A day later she didn't know who we were and we had her put to sleep. That was 18 months before I met Pea, but the weight of the anguish and pain surrounding her passing hadn't lessened in that time.

I wasn't prepared for the grief that hit me. For 12 years Lily had been a divine gift, helping me through over a decade of traumatic events in my life. She would stay near me when I was ill and often sit on the areas of my body that hurt, chirruping and purring. She made me smile and laugh and took me out into the garden on days when I could barely get out of bed. I showered her with affection and gratitude in return. She kept my heart open when it so wanted to close down. The anguish of not finding out what was wrong with her, the guilt over what we put her through and the pain of her loss were so huge that I went into a state of existential angst, but I couldn't share it with anyone and was at some level ashamed of not being able to get over it.

At the Glasgow workshop with Amelia, subconsciously I was looking to heal and consciously I wanted to see if I could communicate with animals. On the first day of the workshop my back was agony and I was feeling very scared. The minute Amelia began to speak about animals I had to stifle the most enormous sobs and to avoid embarrassing myself I went and hid at the back. If I could have run away I would have done so, but my back wouldn't let me. I felt so lonely and beyond help, and then Pea sat next to me and held my hand. Her presence was immediately calming and grounding. The authenticity of her love and concern was tangible. Up to that point I had felt so alone in my grief and suddenly I felt completely seen and understood. After months of hoping Lily's spirit lived on but not being able to believe it, I was so comforted to hear Pea quite matter of factly describing her and saying things my heart had longed to hear: that she was fine and loved me still and that I had to let go of the guilt. I hadn't said anything to Pea about myself, Lily or how I felt. What was so powerful was the way she came across as really down to earth and full of integrity. There was no doubt she was communicating with Lily. It was just the shock needed to shut my logical mind up. I took Pea's card away with me and a month later she did a reading with Lily and Angelica, my other cat.

After that, my whole perception began to shift, my heart began to heal and my relationship with Angelica, which had been distant whilst Lily was alive, began to turn into something beautiful. She is now one of my greatest teachers.

A year later I attended several workshops with Pea that were wonderful and I know now that my path is animal communication and healing.

❧ 'Mr Jones Wants to Speak with You' ❧

On the second day of the workshop, something even more surprising happened and it was all I could do to stop myself falling off my chair. (I can confidently say this wasn't because of the gin and tonics the night before.) We were just about to go into the afternoon break when Amelia took me by complete surprise.

'Pea, Mr Jones wants to speak with you. Would you like to speak with him?'

I had been asked by the dearly departed and world-famous cat of the most inspirational animal communicator, bestselling author and international speaker, a woman I greatly admired, whether I would like to communicate with him. Would I like to? Well, do cats like to purr and knead their paws?

'Yes, I would love to,' I replied in a mixture of complete disbelief and nervousness.

Once all the other people had gone off for coffee or were busying themselves in the room, I took a seat at the front opposite Amelia and she passed me Mr Jones' photograph, along with a piece of paper with questions she'd prepared to ask him. I reminded myself to breathe and looked lovingly into his eyes. Connecting with him felt very easy. I am sure he was doing all the hard work; all I had to do was sit and listen. The room fell silent and I lost all awareness of everyone but Mr Jones and Amelia. It was as if we were submerged underwater in our very own bubble.

I began by describing what I sensed to be Mr Jones' character, because I wanted to make sure I was connecting with the right cat! Luckily, everything made sense to Amelia, so we continued with her questions and I began relaying Mr Jones' responses. I didn't know whether this was a test or whether she genuinely wanted to hear what he had to say through someone else's connection. I also didn't really want to think about this too much because I knew it would just end up blocking me and it might all go pear-shaped.

Then, out of nowhere, I heard a louder, more abrupt voice answering one of the questions.

'Oh no, that's Flo,' Amelia grinned.

Flo was Amelia's other beloved cat, also in spirit. Her voice was loud and clear and drowned out poor Mr Jones. Amelia must have known her other fur-angel would get in on the act, because she was holding another piece of paper with 'Flo' written at the top.

'No pressure then,' I joked with her. *This is no ordinary client*, I thought. *I am sitting here with the most amazing animal communicator on the planet and have been given questions to ask Flo, of all cats. Flo! Immortalized in Amelia's second book,* The Language of Miracles.

'I'd better not get this wrong,' I said with a mountain of trepidation.

'Just say the very first thing. It's lightning fast,' Amelia said, completely deadpan. And so that's what I did. No editing, no questioning – I just received the information and then I said it. And do you know what? It worked.

'Ask Flo what's the colour of her favourite cushion,' said Amelia.

'Ruby red,' I heard before she'd even finished asking the question.

'Yes, that's exactly right. It's actually pink, but Flo always calls it ruby red.'

Phew! Suddenly I felt like a kid who'd been given an A+. What amazed me with this experience was not only what an honour it was, which of course I acknowledge – never in my wildest dreams would I have thought I would be asked by Mr Jones and Amelia to communicate with him, let alone Flo – but how calm I felt, because of Amelia's very clever words: 'Just say the very first thing. It's lightning fast.' That's what I will always remember about this experience and what I take with me into every challenging situation.

A few years later Amelia gave me a gift. 'I want you to have this,' she said, offering me Flo's tiny ruby-red cushion. I keep it safe on my mantelpiece.

🐾 *The Final Curtain* 🐾

Two weeks after the Glasgow workshop I was sitting in a small white-washed rehearsal room over the low rumbles of the circle and district lines of Sloane Square tube station in central London. On the large desk in front of me was my script and stacks of hi-tech sound equipment. Across the room was a smaller desk with an old fashioned reel-to-reel recorder and behind it was a man sitting in an electric wheelchair. He had thin grey strands of hair combed over his liver-spotted and tanned head, large confident hands and a beguiling smile. He was one of the most respected (and often feared) playwrights of the previous five decades, also an accomplished director and actor. Now over 70 years old, he still retained a sharpness and intellect that would defeat anyone from Mensa. Harold Pinter was rehearsing his role in a one-man play called *Krapp's Last Tape*.

We were in the middle of rehearsals when I heard the director, Ian Rickson, say my name.

'Pea has actually stopped working in the theatre, Harold, and now works with animals. We're lucky to have her.'

'Really?' said Harold. 'In what capacity? What do you do with them?'

'I communicate with them,' I said, my legs began to shake under the table as I wondered how Harold would respond. 'I try to understand them, so I can help them.'

'How interesting,' he said, and then, after a Pinter-pause, 'well, the very best of luck to you.'

'Thank you,' I smiled. This was a poetic moment I will always treasure. I had worked with Harold on a number of shows over the previous five years and had come to like him, really like him, as a human being. It was a blessing to have this moment of transition from one career to another with one of the people I most respected and admired.

I can safely say this was the turning point when I became a *bona fide* professional animal communicator and a retired stage manager. In my heart, at this moment I started one of the most exciting, challenging and satisfying rides of my life. 'Weren't you scared?' people ask me. No, I felt excited about making the move from the theatre into animal communication. I didn't ask too many 'What on earth am I doing?' type questions. It just felt natural. What I had been waiting for. It was meant to be.

And I felt great.

❧ *Spreading the Word* ❧

During the 2006 Glasgow workshop Amelia and I had shared a conversation about teaching. 'I've been thinking about teaching workshops,' I'd said. Amelia had responded really positively – in her eyes the more people that knew about animal communication, the better. She had felt I was ready and had been very encouraging.

In retrospect my conversation with Amelia was what I had been looking for – a sign that I was on the right path. I felt I was being guided towards teaching. I wanted to be able to share the joy of animal communication with as many people as possible and I knew it was a powerful way to help animals. Animal communication workshops can change the lives of animals and people too. I am an example of this.

I didn't waste any time. As soon as I arrived back in London I began to plan and over the next couple of months I began to formulate my material. I had piles of paper scattered all over my office and countless reference books by my side. Many drafts later I came up with a schedule for a one-day workshop. That seemed the easy part, the fun part. Now it was time to memorize the material so I could present it without constantly referring to my notes.

This part was daunting, but even more frightening was that I discovered I had no voice. Not in the obvious sense that I couldn't speak, but in a more abstract way. As I began to read my notes out loud I felt really uncomfortable hearing my own voice. It was as though it was alien to me. I couldn't believe how awkward I felt. When I had worked as a company stage manager it was my responsibility to run the technical rehearsals. These involved all technical aspects of the production coming together to create the lighting, sound, projection, video, pyrotechnics, props, scene changes, you name it. All these different aspects came together at the same time the actors were on stage working through the play. Obviously with so many things happening it would take a lot of practice to co-ordinate what the director and creative team wanted. My job would be to manage this process so that we could stop, reset and go again as quickly as possible. I also organized the stage management and stage crew to enable the scene changes to go faultlessly and quickly. It will be no surprise that I had to use my voice a lot to communicate effectively.

So what on earth was happening to me now? I had stood in front of very influential directors, actors and designers and had also cued *The Fast Show* at Hammersmith Apollo, which was *really* fast, but the idea of standing up in front of people I knew to hold a trial workshop was scary. Some people on the spiritual circuit might say I was learning to 'speak my truth', and maybe this is true. I was certainly learning to talk about a subject that at best people had never heard of and at worst had dismissed or ridiculed as make-believe. I had to literally stand up for what I believed in, and as this was my first time public speaking in this way, it didn't feel a comfortable place to stand. I'd spent 15 years standing silently in the darkness of the theatre wings, but now I was forcing myself to stand on the stage.

I was determined to get it right. I purchased a flipchart stand and roll of paper and wrote some points out so I could provide visual information for the students as well as prompts for myself. But over the course of the next few days I kept forgetting what I wanted to say and I got worse and worse until I'd worked myself up into quite a state and pronounced, 'I don't think I can do this.' That was when help came to my rescue in a form I didn't expect.

It was Friday night, the evening before the scheduled workshop. I was standing at the flipchart stand in despair. Everything had been arranged: the venue, the students, the guest teachers and the refreshments. All I had to do was turn up and deliver, but I was frozen with fear.

Then Morgan, who'd introduced me to animal communication in the first place, walked into the room. He took one look at my face and then laid his warm canine body over my feet. This was very strange – he'd never done this before. Within a few minutes I felt a calm descend over me. All the panic, all the upset, all the dread simply disappeared, to be replaced by the most relaxing sensation of stillness, calm and certainty that it would all be all right. I exhaled a welcome sigh and put my notes down. At that moment I just knew I didn't need to look at them anymore. Morgan had worked some kind of magic. I felt completely capable and ready.

Aware of the difference, Morgan walked out the room and back to his bed. I packed up my things ready for the morning, had a bath and treated myself to a glass of wine.

Saturday morning came and I arrived at a house that is often hired out as a filming studio. I felt it was important to get out of my own home and hold this practice workshop at a location I didn't know so it could be more like the real thing. Four friends came to be my students. I had a 50/50 split: two students who had done a little bit of communication before and two who hadn't done any. Within this small group was also a professional teacher, as well as a TV producer used to working with presenters. It wasn't the easiest class, but I was keen to receive honest feedback from people qualified to comment.

Even though I felt a little nervous on the day, the workshop went well. Everyone was able to communicate, including the two people who had never done it before. There were animal guest teachers throughout the day, two dogs and a rabbit, and also animal communication using photographs. The professional teacher, who I thought might be a challenge, because he was so logical and analytical, was actually an excellent student. He discovered he was able to communicate with his family tortoise, who was over 50 years old and living with his parents in the north of the country. Even more remarkably, the lady who had looked as though she was suffering the most awful hangover when she'd first arrived had made a full recovery by the end. She was energized, excited and bowled over by the evidence that she could communicate too.

While I may take some credit for the workshop's success, I wonder how much of it was actually due to Morgan. Throughout the day he was downstairs listening and I wonder whether he was working his magic again. On breaks he pottered round us and looked as though he was checking to see if we were all OK.

I'd asked him whether he'd mind being a teacher in the afternoon and he was scheduled before the tea break. My friend took him out for a walk after lunch, timing it so he would be back for his guest-teaching spot, but Morgan had other ideas. On the walk back he quickened up the pace until my friend was virtually running down the street with him. He seemed to know when he was due on, but what he didn't realize was that *I* was running late. As soon as he was in the door and off the lead, he was climbing up the stairs to be with us – strange, as he hadn't been interested in coming up in the slightest the rest of the day. Bless his heart, he walked into the group and announced, 'I'm here.' I apologized and explained that I was behind schedule and he very reluctantly went back downstairs.

Ten minutes later he was up again and doing a wonderful job connecting with everyone. He told us that his favourite food was, in fact, Texas' food. That didn't surprise me because he loves eating foods he knows he shouldn't even more than his own. It's as though he feels he's pulled a fast one.

There was one student who felt she knew him really well and initially she didn't even try to connect with him, but when I rephrased the question to, 'What is his favourite food *today*?', it freed up her logical mind and she sailed on through the rest of the questions.

He also showed the students his favourite walk in a wood and explained that he wasn't really into toys; they just didn't do anything for him unless a treat was attached. Like many animals on my workshops, he also took the opportunity to make a request: more than one student heard him say he wanted *another* bed, to take his total to four. He really was a star teacher, keen to make sure everyone had proof they could 'do it'.

At the end of the workshop the students felt exhilarated and so did I. We were all buzzing and toasting each other with champagne.

This was the beginning of my journey teaching animal communication to others. The thought of being able to share this ability to help animals to live happier lives and to ease their suffering was deeply satisfying. The animals' guardians would also find the answers to the questions they craved to ask. I could feel myself living a life that felt so right for me. And to have this empowering experience on my birthday was just the icing on the cake!

CHAPTER 7

Animals Have Souls

'DO ANIMALS GO TO HEAVEN?' 'Do their souls continue beyond death?' 'Will I ever see them again?' 'Can they reincarnate?' These are questions I am often asked. Before I discovered animal communication I believed death was it. The end. After death there was nothing. I was so terrified of death I wouldn't let anyone talk about it in my company. If they continued regardless, it wouldn't be long before I was a quivering wreck in floods of tears, because in my mind I knew death was final. In death you no longer existed. This is why it is even more amazing that some of my favourite communications have been with animals who have passed over ... and even come back.

❖ *HRH Riki* ❖

Back in January 2006 I discovered Riki when I was scrolling through the messages on an animal forum website called Canine Health Concern and came across a plea from Lynne in Yorkshire. Coincidentally, we had joined the forum on the same day. Lynne was appealing for help for her Spinone, Riki, who was still grieving for his best mate, Bramble, who had died three years earlier. I had an incomprehensible urge to contact her and offer my help. I have only done this on one other occasion; the other animal was Mono.

Dogs come in all shapes and sizes and Riki was no exception. The first time I held his photo I broke into a big smile. I was looking at a photo of a leggy and rugged Wookie. Long ears dangled down beyond his jaw, flat against a very large, bony head.

'Who are you calling bony?' he interrupted.

Riki is a member of the Italian Spinone tribe.

'Italiano Spi-no-nay,' he pronounced.

His fur was the colour of washed tropical sands. To the untrained eye he could be confused with a large sheep. As I looked at his photo, I imagined sinking my hands into those creamy wisps.

'Riki, if I were to compare you to an Italian male, who would you suggest?' I asked.

'Just compare me to the Pope – he's the guy in the white nightie,' he replied.

Fur cascaded over his eyes down to a soggy old-man goatee below. It might have appeared he was finding it hard to see. But he saw all right. He saw right into your soul.

'God, you're cute.' I said.

Unusual human-like eyes smiled back; the unique Spinone round shape. 'You're not so bad yourself.'

And with that one look and grin, I was hooked. I introduced myself and asked Riki if he would like to talk.

'Sure,' he said, not at all fazed.

Pen in hand, I started to ask him about Bramble.

'Bramble was my best mate,' he began. 'I loved him with all my heart. He is still present in my house – not always, but sometimes. When he's not here I miss him.'

I could feel emptiness inside, as though something was missing. Bramble had also been a member of the Spinone tribe and although he and Riki had not been blood brothers, it felt as though they might as well have been. I sensed Bramble had died very quickly, rather than from a long-term illness.

'Bramble was kicked in the jaw,' Riki continued with a heavy sadness. 'That man broke his jaw and broke his spirit. But I mended his heart. We are forever united by our hearts' connection. I cared for him all his life. He was very ill and in pain most of the time. I would cheer him up and we would have fun together.'

Riki then told me he loved chicken. And he started to talk about Lynne and told me to tell her exactly what he said – word for word:

Lynne worries too much. She needs to calm down and find some love for herself. She revolves her life around me and I only want her to be happy. Focus on your own health more, Lynne, and mine will improve. I am a mirror to your soul. You are the most loving and generous woman and I am always very grateful we came together. It was our intended journey to meet and live with one another. You have a big heart of love and you are learning to take care of dogs in need both emotionally and physically. Bramble is with us. I feel a deep sadness of loss inside you that needs to be healed. You have had a lot to deal with.

I relayed Riki's message and a few days later Lynne e-mailed me. She was stunned that a dog could be so wise and so knowing. She was also relieved to know that Bramble was still around, as that was the first time anyone had mentioned to her that animals live on in spirit, and she was amazed by the accuracy of what Riki had said – she told me that she'd been to more than your average amount of funerals in a very short time.

However, she also told me, 'No, he can't eat chicken or turkey. He's intolerant to them – they give him really bad colitis.'

Nevertheless, a few days later she was tempted to cook some chicken for him, just in case. Leaving it on the side to cool, she went to answer the phone. By the time she got back, he'd eaten it.

'I'd waited nearly 11 years and wasn't prepared to wait any longer!' Riki retorted. From that time on he was able to enjoy cooked chicken without any ill-effects.

He continued:

We are all here together to learn from one another and to grow on our intended path. There is no start and no end. We live here and now. This is our moment and unless we live it with an open heart

and a face full of fun, what's the point? I love you dearly, Lynne –
please listen to what I say as I guide you towards your chosen path.
We are here together intentionally. Bramble was a great gift. He
came to teach you, but you still have a lot to learn. What do you
feel you are learning? There is no untruth. Learn to love yourself
the way I see and love you! You are a beautiful soul that needs to
fly free. You can release your chains simply by your intention. Be
true.

A week later Lynne e-mailed again, concerned about some
sore eruptions on Riki's legs. I offered to channel some distant
healing to him. Sometimes as I did this I could feel within my
own body what Riki was feeling in his – the position of his
sores, his tender right shoulder and very sore lower back. My
hands felt rooted to these two spots, like the sturdiest tree in
a storm. Once the healing energy subsided, I e-mailed Lynne
to tell her what I'd felt and she decided to mention it at the
visit to the vet's that was scheduled for later that week.

Afterwards she wrote to me:

> The vet confirmed Riki's right shoulder was slacker than usual and
> since his fall from grace on the laminate flooring last May he does
> have lower back problems. To be honest, these last couple of days
> it was me that could have done with the Reiki. I've suffered with
> slipped discs for over 30 years now.

I began to piece together some of the meaning in Riki's
message. He wanted Lynne to focus on her own healing, and

as well as this, it appeared some of his own physical discomfort matched hers.

She expanded:

> My main problem area is the very bottom of my back, probably the last two or three vertebrae, which I think is very similar to Riki's problem – almost a mirror image. I have even had to make Riki's walks a bit shorter these past few weeks because of it.

In the beginning Riki was understanding and accepted the shorter walks, but it wasn't long before he started to get really brassed off and I was asked to start to channel Reiki to Lynne too. Four sessions later she reported that her back felt 'pretty much all right again now'. With help from the homoeopathic vets Chris Day and John Saxon, Riki's sores began to heal too and fur started to sprout again. At the same time he started to lift out of the grief he'd been feeling for three years and his cheekier, happier side showed itself. Lynne and I jokingly called him HRH, His Royal Highness, because he liked to be waited on hand and foot.

It wasn't long after this that Riki made his first request: he stipulated that Lynne should learn Reiki. He wanted her to be able to heal herself. He also wanted her to begin to heal him and other animals. He saw this as her future once he was gone.

Lynne felt it made sense. She'd had a couple of friends suggest she take up Reiki, but to hear Riki request it confirmed it was right. The main problem was finding a Reiki

Master, but within two searches she had located a lady just half an hour away.

'That made me think of what someone once said: if you're meant to do Reiki, then Reiki will find you,' she said.

🐾 *Riki's Message to Lynne* 🐾

As the spring daffodils began to burst, I sat in the garden surrounded by their cheerful sunshine petals. Lynne had asked me to connect with Riki and an image of him jumped up with his paws either side on my shoulders, his eyes looking directly into mine, full of love and smiles.

Riki asked for more fish, saying the oils would help with his dry skin. He said that meant more 'sardines, mackerel and salmon'. He said no to shampoo and he wanted the flowers in the white china vase to be left on the unit between the TV and fireplace because they were beautiful.

'Would you like to go and see the holistic vet, Riki?' I asked Lynne's first question.

'Geography, calligraphy,' he said.

What? Why was he spurting random words at me?

'Are you having a laugh?' I quizzed him.

'Yes! She takes it all far too seriously. Lynne needs to focus less on my health and more on her own, but she's in denial, not willing to look inside herself. I only want her to be happy and I know she's not. I don't mean to be cruel, but sometimes I just feel like shaking her.'

I could feel his frustration, but I wanted to persevere with the questions. 'Lynne wants to know whether you'd like to go and see your homoeopathic vet,' I tried a second time.

'I always want to visit him because he is a nice man. Can he work on Lynne instead? I will go with her to keep her company. Everything helps, but *I am the wrong patient*. Ask her to ask herself, "What's wrong with this picture?" Ask her these questions: What am I trying to teach you? Why is your own health not as important as mine? Why do you value yourself so low, when I see you floating in the clouds like an angel? When will it all stop? When will you have given enough? Ask her to see herself as I see her. She holds on to her pain and she puts all her focus elsewhere, because she does not want to take the brave step of releasing it. I am not drawing the pain away, Lynne. I am showing you how much discomfort you have. I want you to release it. I love you and I am here to help you become the beautiful soul that you are.'

I blew out a huge sigh. 'Do you have anything else to say?' I asked tentatively.

'Not just now. She'll find that very hard to hear.'

🐾 *Riki's Secret* 🐾

Through our regular communication sessions, Riki and I very quickly became firm friends, connected 24 hours a day, 7 days a week, 365 days a year. I'm not suggesting he was bugging me every second, suggesting this or that, but he was there rain or shine, being my guide, my teacher, my rock, my stand-up comic, my fearless defender and above all my friend.

As autumn arrived, he shared a secret with me. 'I'll be coming back,' he said, 'tell Lynne I am coming back and she is to look for me again.'

He was declaring he would reincarnate and come back to Lynne. I felt excited.

'How will she know where to find you?' I said, picking up my pen.

'I'm going to tell you. I will be a girl. Female. I am going to be the runt of the litter – this is very important. I will be with a breeder, but not a normal breeder – this breeder also rescues animals. I will rush forward and bite the little finger on Lynne's left hand. Little finger, left hand.'

'Where is this breeder?'

Riki gave me a direction, northeast, but that was it.

'Is there anything else?'

'Yes, tell Lynne that I will love pink. I will want lots of pink. I want her to get more in touch with her feminine side. That's why I'm coming back as a girl.'

I e-mailed the details and a rapid flurry of messages ensued.

Lynne was astounded and not convinced. 'I would never get a bitch,' she wrote. 'Riki knows that. I've always had boys.'

'I'm sorry, Lynne, he was really clear on this. He's coming back as a girl,' I e-mailed back. 'And he says he's going to be a puppy.'

'No! I can't have a puppy. What *is* he thinking? I'd love him to come back, but I have to think of my age, and I've never had a puppy. In fact I had almost reached the decision not to have another dog at all, but it looks now as though the decision has been overruled. I've no problem at all with Riki returning as another Spinone, though. The breed is wonderful. Do you think at some point he could be more specific? Will he communicate with you when he's ready to appear and send a route map?'

That I didn't know.

🐾 'You're Here' 🐾

It was Christmas 2006 when I went to visit Riki and Lynne at their home in Yorkshire. As I pulled into the drive Riki was already waiting for me on the doorstep.

'You're here,' I said out loud.

'Yes. And so are you,' he replied silently.

I reached out and sunk my hands into his deep shag-pile fur, surprised at how rugged and harsh it felt, then kissed the top of his head. He smelled of wild moors and heather. He was even more striking in real life – a golden Chewbacca with veiled eyes.

Lynne said, 'I've been mulling over what he said to you about coming back as a female puppy and begun to think of names. One name really screamed at me: Phoenix.'

After supper we nestled in front of the TV and waited in anticipation of watching one of Riki's favourite programmes. For the past half-hour he'd been lying only inches away from the front of the screen. *You've Been Framed* was the highlight of his week. Lynne told me if he was in the car and thought he was going to miss it, he'd get into a blind panic and will Lynne to drive faster. If for any reason it wasn't screened, he'd insist she flick through the channels and check with the set upstairs, and then he'd proceed to be really puzzled all evening.

He also liked *Pet Rescue*, but wasn't bothered by any other animal programmes. Film-wise, he would settle happily in front of *Home Alone 2*, *Whistle Down the Wind* and *The Thorn Birds*. There's no accounting for taste.

'Turn it on, we can't miss the start,' he demanded now, his eyes playing table tennis between Lynne and me.

In order to enjoy the programme to the full, Riki took the best seat in the house, lying directly in front of the telly, his nose almost pressing against the screen. He laughed throughout, turning round occasionally to check whether we'd got the joke. 'Did you see that?!' he'd say, cracking up, mouth open wide, eyes smiling, as little wriggles of excitement and pleasure rippled down his spine. Then he'd quickly turn back to the screen, eyes fixed forward again. He laughed the most when the humans did silly things and made fools of themselves.

Once his programme was over Riki ambled out to the dining room and lay by the treat cupboard. Lynne offered him a chew stick, but he wasn't impressed. She gave up and left me to it.

'You're the animal communicator, you have a go,' she said, retreating to the kitchen.

I suddenly realized he'd done this to get Lynne out of the way, because as soon as we were alone he stood and walked over to me with purpose in his stride, then gave me his sternest Paddington Bear stare.

'What is it, Riki?' I asked, concerned. He was normally grinning, so this was a new side to him.

'You have to promise me you'll get Lynne to your workshop,' he said.

The coming summer I would be teaching an animal communication workshop in Yorkshire. I had hoped Lynne would attend, but she was insisting she couldn't come because Riki wouldn't be able to make the stairs and there was nowhere within eyeshot he could rest.

'Promise me,' he demanded.

'I promise, Riki,' I said in all sincerity. I didn't know how I was going to achieve it, but having made a promise to Riki I knew I had to keep it. He hardly ever asked things of me, and never with such seriousness. This was important to him.

'I will be coming too,' he said. 'I want to teach and I have a question I want you to ask me.'

'What is your question?'

'What is the meaning of life?'

'And what *is* the meaning of life, Riki?'

Then he told me and said he wanted to reveal it to everyone in the workshop.

❧ *Riki's Workshop* ❧

The time for the workshop came round and by an amazing turn of events the original venue closed, which meant I had to find a new location. I web searched and was drawn to a barn near Halifax. Oddly, Lynne knew of it and the lady who ran it. Riki's wish was granted: Lynne agreed to attend and would bring him as a guest teacher.

My 'Mother Mary', who is called Mary and is a mother to me in every way except blood, was coming over from Leeds to help me with the hospitality side of the workshop and offered to 'Riki sit' while Lynne was being a student inside. It was an intensely hot day and they settled themselves underneath a beautifully constructed sunshade.

Once the workshop began I felt a sort of super-energy running through me. I began to relax and forgot about my snuffly cold. In a blink of an eye it was lunchtime. Riki's starring moment wasn't until the afternoon, but he received visits in every break, as well as one-on-one devotion from Mary, who accompanied him whenever he fancied a walkabout. I sat with him at lunchtime and we had a chat of our own.

'Are you helping me?' I quizzed him.

'What if I am?' he grinned.

'Just make sure you're OK. Don't get too hot and tired.'

He grinned an even bigger grin back at me.

'Are you sure you're able to stay?' I pushed.

'Stop fussing. I'm staying.' He could be incorrigible.

After lunch, it was Riki's moment. We left the barn and sat on the ground around him. He was lying down under his sunshade with all the pomp and ceremony of a king. He looked way too hot, but told me not to draw attention to it. He wanted to teach without any distractions.

One by one Riki patiently answered the questions we presented to him and the students came up with stunningly accurate answers. He was a clear and direct teacher, able to touch hearts in a simple yet profound way. It was very humbling watching him weave his magic despite his physical discomfort in the sweltering heat.

We'd got to the end of the list and it was time to ask the most important question. I addressed the group. 'Riki would like you to ask him this question: what is the meaning of life?'

These were the messages the students received from him:

'To love one another.'

'To love all beings.'

'To give love unconditionally to all people and animals.'

'Sharing love.'

'Being loving to one another.'

'To love unconditionally.'

Finally I repeated the answer Riki had given me six months earlier: '*Love.*'

❧ *Do All Good Things Really Come to an End?* ❧

The next morning I received terrible news. Riki had been strong and held on until he'd shared his message, but then the heat had taken control and he had collapsed.

By a string of coincidences Lynne was helped getting Riki from the workshop to their home. She spent a couple of hours rehydrating him and getting his temperature down.

She wrote to me: 'He had it the way he wanted and planned, but it's taken so much out of him, more I think than he anticipated.'

This felt like the beginning of the end. Riki had given a hint the previous Christmas that he'd keep going until the workshop, but then afterwards he would be happy to ascend. 'Job done,' he'd said.

I knew he was preparing to leave, but all week I was still hit by an illogical grief.

Lynne, on the other hand, was feeling a sense of calm and acceptance. On the Friday she rang. 'Riki asked me to tell you, "Pea is sad. Tell her not to be. I'm not going anywhere, just my body. I'll always be at Lynne's side, but Bramble will need to shove over a bit. I want a celebration of my life – laughter, not tears. Wear your brightest colours and be happy. I'll be happy. We'll be having a party, all my pals and the ice-cream man."'

I smiled. Riki knew I was a massive fan of ice cream. Lynne didn't. He'd mentioned it to make sure his message connected with me, and it did.

❧ *Protected by Angels* ❧

For two days Riki was exhausted. Lynne asked me to see how he was feeling and I was able to confirm what she herself had sensed: 'He is ready to go now. But first he would like to say goodbye to some of his friends.'

During the time he had left, Riki somehow managed to say goodbye to everyone that was important to him. One by one, dogs he hadn't seen for months were suddenly there again – Jake and Billy, Mollie, Millie and Chubs – and his human friends appeared too. Lynne's son Damian battled through flooding and severe train delays to be by his side.

A couple of days before Riki ascended, a calm cloaked me and I joined Lynne in acceptance. I knew Riki was in control of his ascension, just as he had been in control of all the cogs and levers of his life. He had left nothing to chance: he had given clear instructions about flowers, candles and even the music he wanted – 'Protected by Angels'. He had given Lynne and me the picture of yellow daffodils, but it was the wrong time of year, so he had to settle for yellow oriental lilies.

He was ready to ascend, but there was one more person he wanted to see. He gave me the image of one of his vets, and Lynne said this would be Eddy, his favourite vet for the past 12 years. That morning Riki told her it was time to ring him. Eddy said he couldn't get over until 2 p.m., but Riki said he'd wait. Once Eddy had arrived to say goodbye and Riki had thanked him, he was happy and just let go. He flew solo, peacefully and without medical assistance. Just as he was the driver in his life, so he was the driver in his death. I wasn't with him when he ascended, but from my living room in London, I saw an image of his spirit assisted up to heaven by what felt like an angelic presence and his old pal Bramble. My watch read 2.11 p.m. Without any prompting from me, Lynne later told me that was the exact time Riki had ascended.

A while later, when I was writing Riki's story I asked Lynne if she could express what Riki had given her. This is what she wrote:

It came as quite a shock to be told that, with help, anyone can communicate with animals and I was in denial for some considerable time. So Riki stage-managed things so that I'd have no excuse for not attending an animal communication workshop. He ensured a change from the intended venue and sorted a new one a mere 20 minutes away. Not only that, he organized a minder for himself.

Life after that workshop has never been the same. Riki was able to tell me when he was ready to pass over and when to ring the vet he still needed to say goodbye to. I still receive messages from him now, even though his body has gone. He keeps me firmly rooted to the path that he wants me to follow.

Communication with Riki is wonderful, but just the tip of the iceberg. I'm now able to help other animals and their guardians with their worries and concerns, and lighten their load. He's ensured that I've met people able to expand my knowledge of alternative therapies and able to attune me to Reiki so that I can give healing to others. He's turned my belief systems upside down. I know now that animals survive death and are always there for us, no matter what their form. Special also is the knowledge that animals aren't 'dumb' – they are teachers and guides. And to still talk to Riki? Priceless!

❧ *The Phoenix Rises* ❧

Riki wasn't away for long. Seven months earlier he'd given me the details: he'd come back as a girl puppy, the runt of the litter, from a rescue centre that also bred animals, and it would be easy to be certain it was him because when he met Lynne again he'd bite the little finger on her left hand.

One day she switched on her computer and heard Riki in his spirit form say, 'Google Spinone litters. Look at the first listing at the top. Check the details.'

Lynne rang me, very excited:

I now understand the location. He guided me to the breeder and once I looked at the location I realized it was just a few hundred yards from where he was born. When I clicked on the home page there was music playing: 'Can You Feel the Love Tonight?' That was one of our favourite songs.

I rang them up, but the breeder said all the puppies were spoken for.

I said, 'Are you sure? Are you sure you don't have one left for me? How about the runt?'

The line went quiet and then she said, 'How do you know there's a runt?'

'Just a hunch,' I told her.

Then she said, 'Well … we do have a runt, but we were going to have to keep her.'

So I've made an appointment to go and meet her …

After the visit Lynne rang me again. She was like a shaken champagne bottle about to pop:

Kerrie and I climbed out of the car and heard a puppy squealing and just knew it was Phoenix. The squealing continued as I walked into the living room where there were two wire pens about four feet high separating the cream and orange puppies from the cream and brown ones.

The screaming carried on as I walked over to the pups with Riki's colouring. I was looking at 14 healthy and calm brothers and sisters, but I couldn't see Phoenix. Then all of a sudden a screaming puppy came bursting out from deep at the back, clambered over all the siblings and launched herself to the front of the cage where I was kneeling. After a crashing halt into the wire frame she stood on her back paws, opened her mouth and gave the little finger on my left hand a very gentle nibble. She totally ignored Kerrie, who was kneeling beside me. She tried to climb out of the pen to reach me, and when I picked her up, for the first time since we'd arrived she stopped screaming and there was silence.

I've found him. It's Phoenix.

Lynne was out of breath and I was virtually speechless. Everything checked out: from a breeder who also rescued, a female and the runt of the litter. She had forced her way from the back, past 14 brothers and sisters, to bite Lynne's left hand – on her little finger.

I was grinning from ear to ear. 'He's back!'

❧ *Phoenix/Riki Similarities* ❧

When Phoenix arrived home, it was as though she'd already got a download of the house and a guidebook. She walked straight into the kitchen and stood waiting in between the end of the breakfast bar and the central heating boiler – where Riki had always had his feeding-stand. There weren't any dog bowls there, in fact no doggie things at all.

After Phoenix had finished her supper she crossed the kitchen and sat directly in front of a cupboard that used to house Riki's square biscuits. The cupboard door was still shut and the biscuits were in a sealed packet, but somehow she knew supper wasn't over. She even counted them out: eight square biscuits, i.e. four whole biscuits broken in half – just like Riki.

Lynne sent me a list of further similarities:

- Phoenix lets out a silly high-pitched squeak at the end of her yawn, just like Riki.
- The very first night she was home she lay on the rug by the fire, just like Riki.

- On *his* first night at home Riki must have stretched out quite suddenly, because he hit a ceramic plant pot, pushing it into the fireplace. It smashed and he was terrified. Phoenix did exactly the same thing with the replacement pot.
- Over the first few nights, Phoenix used to lie down behind the sofa, squishing herself in by the wall, just like Riki.
- If there were people visiting whom Riki had been particularly fond of, Phoenix would make a fuss of them, as though they were old friends. With everyone else she'd be very wary and skittish, but with Riki's old friends she felt right at home.
- Riki's closest canine friends were the ones who were anti-dog – the sort of dogs who'd pick a fight, cause trouble, the bolshy ones. They included Chubby, a border collie cross, Billy, a fox terrier cross who has major attitude, and Cody, a Labrador. Phoenix was accepted by them all straight away, without any 'getting to know you period'. When they met it looked as though they were welcoming her back. They approached with tails wagging tentatively, gave her a good sniff and then had tails whirring like helicopter blades. They were ecstatic – there was absolutely no mistaking it. They already knew her. Titch, an elderly female smooth collie cross who's normally very nervous of other dogs, accepted Phoenix the moment they met.

There were so many similarities, it was hard to ignore that Phoenix had some of Riki's knowledge. One thing was different, though: Phoenix was crazy about pink. Riki wasn't – and Lynne hated it. But Phoenix picked out a pink collar in a pet shop, put her paw on a pink fleece, preferred to sniff pink flowers and her favourite toys were all … pink!

❧ *Phoenix Becomes a Star* ❧

The first time I met Phoenix was when she was a guest teacher on a Yorkshire workshop at the same venue where Riki had taught.

It was a cold day as I walked out of the barn, down the stairs and into the car park. I rounded the corner and found myself looking at a large dog in the boot of a silver car. I saw Lynne standing close by. I gazed at the beautiful animal inside, looking into gentle, inquisitive eyes with saggy lower lids revealing pink flesh. Then Phoenix jumped down out of the car and made a beeline for me, almost knocking me over. I couldn't believe she was already up to my thighs. She was huge for a year-old puppy, and powerful. Her coat was smooth and silky, different from Riki's, and I loved running my hands down her long velvet ears. As I looked into her eyes I saw a glimpse of Riki, then she gave me his wide-mouthed grin and her eyes twinkled.

'Hi, Riki!' I said, and she grinned even more.

Being a younger, stronger and, let's not forget, female model, Phoenix is of course different. She is part Riki. Or should that read 'Riki is part Phoenix'? Phoenix's energy is sweet, light and playful. She's nervous of motorbikes and cars, but fearless when it comes to cliff edges. Riki was neither.

Phoenix doesn't like getting into the boot of a car, whereas Riki had no problem with it. Apart from the exception of Riki's previous friends, Phoenix likes dogs but not until she's spent a minute gauging what they're like. Riki was everyone's friend straight away. Phoenix enjoys food but is a dainty eater. Riki liked to guzzle.

When it came to Phoenix's star turn at the workshop, I wrote her name at the top of the flipchart pad and turned to her for inspiration. I asked her what questions the students could ask her. She stood up from the rug in the centre of the room and looked me straight in the eyes.

'Ask them who I really am,' she said. Her eyes twinkled and I looked back into the eyes of Riki.

I grinned back at him and said, 'Oh, come on. I can't ask that. Be sensible. They're all beginners.'

Riki laughed.

He hadn't changed that much.

CHAPTER 8

Malteser Musgo

Now HERE'S A story that reveals the counselling element of communicating with an animal. This horse had deep-rooted emotional problems which needed to be heard without the pressures of time or expectation. The outcome was startling and dramatic.

It was a cold November afternoon as I drove through the wooden gate of the livery and into the car park. As I climbed out of the warmth of my car, a woman with shoulder-length dark hair came over and introduced herself as Maddi. She was young, only about 24, and once she was closer, I could see she had green eyes, like the green eyes of cats. Secretly, she was feeling scared. Secretly, I was feeling anxious butterflies; this was my first horse-yard consultation. I had very little experience with horses; basically, I could boil it down to a couple of summer horse treks in Ludlow.

Unbeknownst to me, Maddi wasn't sleeping and was terrified I'd tell her there was nothing that could be done, that she'd have to sell her best friend. In her e-mail to me she'd described her horse as 'a bit strange':

> What I mean by that is that I can be riding him and he is fine, then suddenly, without warning, he gallops off with me totally out of control and with no way of stopping him. Then he'll stop, take a breath and carry on normally as if nothing has happened. This is not a daily occurrence and I can't see any pattern to it.

She had already had him checked by a handful of experts. The vet and saddler had been out a couple of times. An equine physiotherapist had visited and Maddi had also tried equine osteopaths, McTimoney practitioners and massage therapists. Now, somewhere around £1,000 out of pocket, she'd called in an animal communicator. She'd explained:

> He behaves like this at home and at dressage shows. There's no pattern to it. I have got to the point where I don't know what to do with him. Some days he's unsafe to ride; he obviously isn't right in some way. I'm told he's naughty, because no one can find anything physically wrong with him. I feel so distraught. What am I supposed to do with a horse like this? If I'm forced to sell him, I'd worry about what someone else would do to him if his behaviour carries on. I'm at a total loss. I would really like to understand why he is like this, because he is so special. He's polite and good-natured in the stable. If I could do something to make his life better, I would.

Despite a four-year relationship with Musgo, or 'Mus' as Maddi sometimes called him, he'd been unable to settle. She'd asked me down to Kent for a face-to-face yard visit, seeing me as her last resort.

Prior to coming I'd requested Musgo's photo and had communicated with him distantly. Communicating with a horse distantly is quite different from communicating in person. Apart from their daunting height, there's their mood to consider – whether they want to co-operate at the arranged time or whether they'd rather be doing something else instead. There's also the guardian's mood to consider – are they in a good mood, frustrated, sceptic, anxious or scared? Horse yards can be distracting at the best of times, with people noisily mucking out, working with their horses or generally shuffling close by so they can earwig, and I've learned a bit of preparation always helps.

This day was like any other. Young women were wandering around the stables appearing to look busy, but Maddi revealed they were secretly interested and at the same time sceptical about the 'horse communicator' coming to visit.

She led me inside the stable block and down a passage of horses until I reached a stable towards the end on the right and came face to face with Musgo. I wasn't surprised that he appeared completely unperturbed when I said, 'Hi,' over his door – I'd let him know I was coming. He stood like the vision of a grey sky with some dancing wisps of white cloud through his coat. He had cheerless muddy brown eyes, which were slightly hidden behind the lightning flash of his slate-grey mane. Standing there in the corner of his stable, he looked like a shadow of the 11-year old pure-bred Andalusian stallion he could be.

So we could have a little privacy, for Maddi and Musgo as much as myself, I asked if we could go somewhere a little less public. Maddi led us outside to the far end of the car park, out of earshot of the rest of the yard.

As I greeted Musgo he should have reached me at 16.2 hands, which in human terms meant 5 foot 6 inches, my exact height, but instead he felt smaller than me and vulnerable. I prepared myself with a couple of slow deep breaths and sent a feeling of love to him to help him relax. I was concerned about giving him time and space to express himself – what people might compare to a counselling session.

I read out some of the impressions I'd received from Musgo when we'd communicated distantly by his photo: 'I can sense he feels confused and has lots on his mind. He pictured black shin guards. He gave the impression his right side is stretched, from the neck and shoulder down the front right leg. It feels as though pain runs down that right foreleg and sometimes he stamps it, which helps relieve it.'

'Yes, he does stamp it. The right foot,' said Maddi.

'I also feel his muscles are sore from his neck working backwards across the right side of his spine. There's also a spot of soreness in his lower back in the sacral area.'

He'd pictured a block of about 12 stables and now I was here I could see for myself that that was right.

I continued, 'I asked him about his heart and then his lungs and he gave me the impression both were great and he was able to take big deep breaths. Sometimes his stomach is upset, but he indicated this was from nerves rather than any problems with his diet. Finally he brought my attention to his right hip. Everything seems to be a concern on that side. He pictures you leaning to the right and asks if you could sit more central.'

Maddi agreed to be aware of this. 'Can he tell us why he sometimes seems frightened?' she prompted.

'As I'm looking into his face I feel fear. I can feel that he believes "they were coming to get him" to take him away and he was scared,' I said. 'He pictures a trailer and resisting walking into it. He also gives me the feeling he resists being totally controlled.'

'That could make sense. He was sold on to another stud, so someone did take him away. At the first stud he had a wonderful relationship with one of the workers, a man who adored him. Perhaps he wanted to stay there,' said Maddi.

'I can feel a sinking feeling, sadness in my stomach, and he's picturing a dark-haired heavy-set man. He feels like a bully. Musgo's expressing a feeling of weariness. It feels like this man really got him down,' I explained to Maddi.

I tried to soothe Musgo by sending him feelings of gentleness and love. Despite his stature and strength, the handsome stallion in front of us felt scared and sad. It seemed that at some point a man had been unkind to him. I wondered whether it was a groom or someone else working at the new yard.

I turned to Musgo. 'How can we help you?'

'My friend has moved away,' he said. 'I loved him. I am not happy now.'

As he said this he sent me a picture of a black or dark chocolate stallion. The horse came across as older than Musgo. I felt he wasn't just his friend, he was also his protector. As Musgo pictured his friend I could feel his loss.

'We used to have fun together,' he said sadly. Then he pictured himself proudly walking with his friend.

I acknowledged his feeling then asked him Maddi's next question: 'Do you enjoy dressage?'

'I don't know. I don't feel good at it and I'm ugly.'

It was upsetting that he had such a low opinion of himself.

'Find me a new friend. I am lonely,' he said.

'Haven't you got a friend here?'

'No, no friends,' as he pictured the stables behind us.

'I feel his friend was taken away,' I told Maddi. 'They tried to stay together but it wasn't allowed. All of this was before your time with him.'

Maddi was gently nodding her head. 'Does he like me?' she wanted to know. This is a question many people ask their animals.

'Yes, I quite like her, she's kind to me,' came the reply, but in an almost monotonous tone, as though Musgo was talking through a thick fog.

'Could you be happy here?' Maddi said directly to him.

I felt a sinking feeling in my chest as he responded, 'I don't know if I could ever really be happy again.'

Silence filled the air and Maddi was ashen.

'I feel as though my heart's breaking,' she said. 'I find it hard to take in that such a lovely animal is so upset.'

There was a long pause while Maddi composed herself. I waited until she was able to ask her next question.

'Why does he just suddenly take off? I don't understand.'

I put this to Musgo, but he was reluctant to answer. I spent some time slowly reassuring him it was safe for him to tell us and that we were here to support him. Calling on what courage he had left, he was slowly able to answer the question.

'He's picturing someone hitting him,' I explained to Maddi. 'It doesn't feel like his old guardian, it feels as though the guardian is away and it's someone else. This person is hitting him whilst riding him and Musgo doesn't understand why. He calls it "beating" and I can feel he was terrified. This has had a huge effect on him.'

Musgo paused and I could see him frozen in that memory. 'It's all right, Musgo, you're here with us, you're safe now,' I said silently in my mind to him. It was enough to break the moment and help him to recover to tell us more.

'He grew nervous after this and was always worried he'd be hit again. He has flashbacks, and when he has them he wants to be free and to run. He wants to run away.'

Maddi was quiet for a while and then she said, 'I could feel a sense of absolute desperation from Musgo as you were talking.'

'That's right. He's expressing that feeling to both of us,' I confirmed.

Musgo continued, 'I'm scared I'm pushing you away and letting you down. I don't want to do this, because I feel safe with you. You never get angry. I will try and love you and I will try to not run, but you have to understand how hard this is for me.'

Maddi blew out a sigh, 'I feel that there's a glimmer of hope now. If he feels like that, I think that together we can get through this.'

Once Musgo began to share his feelings with us, it seemed to unblock the way for more feelings he'd been holding inside and dealing with all on his own. It felt as though we'd reached a turning-point.

'I miss my partner,' he said. 'We used to train together.'

I wanted to check that his saddle felt comfortable, because horses often complain of sore backs. He pictured a brown saddle with a pad underneath it and gave the impression it was a very comfortable fit. I felt him express that he had a strong back, powerful hind muscles and strong legs. In fact, he felt very fit, but there was a heavy cloak of tiredness and depression weighing him down.

Maddi asked her second question: 'Why does he have difficulty with his left half-pass?'

Half-pass? I wondered to myself. I don't have the honour of sharing my life with a horse, so there are a huge number of horse terms I don't understand. Not to be put off, I went straight to source and asked Musgo to show me what Maddi meant by a half-pass. He pictured himself going round to the left in a small circle then coming to stand where he'd started.

As he pictured this I felt a terrible tight ache in the right side of my neck, a mirror of what he felt in his. When he was pulled to the left there was extra pressure on muscles that felt tight and sore. I could just imagine Maddi practising this move with him and each time the pain gaining in intensity. Standing in front of him, I was able to double-check his neck by a technique similar to X-ray scanning at airports. I sensed hot spots on the right side of his neck, like a red glow, indicating pain or soreness.

'Do you know why your neck is sore?' I said to Musgo.

He pictured falling onto it and then he said, 'Whipped by bully.'

Maddi was taking in every word and detail, and although it felt upsetting for Musgo, I could tell this communication was also therapeutic for him. He needed to be heard, to be understood on this deeper level.

We moved on to Maddi's third question: 'Why can he sometimes do perfect flying changes and passage but at other times he doesn't seem to understand what I'm asking and becomes uptight?'

More horse-terms. I consulted the oracle again: 'Musgo, what does Maddi mean by "flying changes" and "passage"?'

He pictured moving one leg in front of the other with a bit of a hop. 'It's a skip,' he said.

'OK. Why is this a problem?'

Musgo's answer was straightforward. I repeated it for Maddi: 'He finds co-ordination difficult. He has to concentrate really hard. Sometimes he gets frustrated with himself and wants to quit. You pick up on him being uptight, which is correct. It is his frustration you're feeling.'

I asked how we could help Musgo.

'Don't make me practice for so long,' he replied. 'Little and often is better.'

'Musgo feels he has two left feet and finds this more difficult than other things you ask of him,' I reported to Maddi. 'He also finds it harder when he's tired.'

To gain a true reflection of his character I connected with his core self and bypassed the feelings of fear, nerves, low self-esteem and depression. Then I could see a smiley, cheeky horse who liked lots of fun. I could see his boyish good looks and boyish outlook on life. I felt he was very trusting of the farrier and also of people walking behind him.

I asked him, 'What do you like?'

He answered me with a list, which I related to Maddi: 'Carrots, little brown nut-like food from the hand, apples and pears. He's also showing me a purple rug and it's got cream binding. He says he likes this rug.'

'Yes, he has got a purple rug with cream binding, but you'd never know he liked it, he always seems so indifferent to everything,' Maddi said.

'That would make sense because he's feeling down. He hasn't got much interest in anything at the moment.'

When I asked Musgo what help he needed to overcome the issues we'd discussed, I felt Reiki healing and flower essence remedies would be a good start. Instead of locating another Reiki practitioner, Maddi was keen to have continuity and asked me to channel the healing remotely. She agreed to contact a company called Tortue Rouge about suitable flower essence remedies, especially in regard to one of their rem edies called 'Fears'. I also felt it would be helpful for her to boost Musgo's confidence whilst riding him and I asked her to continually tell him he was very handsome and clever.

Right at the end I asked Musgo, 'Is there anything else you'd like?'

In reply I received an image.

'You feed him chocolate,' I stated to Maddi.

'No,' she replied, looking confused.

'What is that?' I pushed Musgo, asking him what it tasted like. As he was showing it to me I described it for Maddi: 'It's small and round. I see chocolate on the outside and it's crunchy on the inside. You gave it to him when he first came to live with you. He calls it "the most delicious thing in the world to eat". He says it comes from a bag and that you like them too. Is it a Malteser?'

Maddi screamed with laughter. 'As soon as you said it came from a bag and I liked them too, I knew it was a Malteser! I love them! Ages ago I gave one to Musgo because he was going mad for it, nudging my hand, which at the time was very unlike him. I can't believe he's remembered that.'

Everyone left the car park more relaxed, but Maddi observed Musgo retreat into the corner of his stable as he'd always done. She walked me through the stable block past her other horse, Thai. She told me the horse next to Thai was being a problem. I paused and made a loving connection with him. I immediately saw the image of a saddle on his back and felt a pinching sensation.

'You might like to suggest the guardian checks his saddle. It doesn't seem to be a perfect fit,' I suggested.

Later on Maddi passed on the message and the guardian immediately stopped using it and agreed to have it refitted or to buy a new one if it was needed.

At the very end of the passage we came to a dejected-looking young bay horse and there was no need to intentionally connect with him, as I was already feeling such a disheartening sadness in my chest as I looked into his eyes. This horse was feeling so low and unloved, he didn't want to be there.

'Whose horse is this?' I said, concerned.

'He's with someone, but I'm not sure they're getting on,' Maddi said.

'Yes, it shows. He's feeling so unhappy. You could help here. Every time you come out to Musgo, try and spend a little time with this guy, telling him how special he is and giving him lots of love and fuss.'

'OK, I will, and I'll let the other girls know too, so we can all fuss him.'

It was hard to leave the sad, sweet horse to walk back to my car, wondering about his future. Sadly, it turned out his guardian sent him back to the trader because they'd decided they didn't like him, causing him to feel a double dose of rejection. I hoped that someone special had noticed the stars in his eyes.

Maddi and I arranged the Reiki appointments for Musgo's distant healing and as we talked Maddi noticed the first sign that Musgo could work through the issues we'd discussed: he was sticking his head out of his window to see what we were doing. For the very first time in four years he was showing an interest. It was a small sign, but it was significant, and Maddi was relieved and thrilled she could already see a change in him.

During the communication Maddi had been fairly quiet, but she struck me as someone who was considerate of others feelings. Sometimes clients have a vast knowledge of the horse world and as I have very little they can be dismissive if I don't express things using the correct terminology. While I was working in the theatre we used a term called 'the iron', which is not what you'd expect – an iron, to iron clothes – but the name for the safety curtain that acts as a fire barrier between the auditorium and stage. To someone who wasn't part of the theatre environment I'd call it the fire curtain, because then that's obvious. When I'm working with horses, if I don't know the correct term I also use an obvious description and hope it's not dismissed just because I'm not part of the horse world. I notice that if accurate information is disregarded, the horse doesn't feel heard and the relationship or issue doesn't improve.

I could tell Maddi had been feeling nervous about what she was going to hear, but she was 100 per cent focused on trying to make Musgo's life happier and understand why he acted the way he did. She'd already read Julie Dicker's book *What Horses Say* and knew that once you understood the problem you had to act on it. She'd admitted she'd been concerned that if Musgo hadn't liked living with her she might have had to find a new guardian for him. It wasn't something she wanted to do because she loved him, but if that had been the cause of the problems she would have done it for his sake. This revealed how brave she was to invite the communication with Musgo and also how committed she was to him. I knew now that they couldn't fail; there was light at the end of Musgo's tunnel of depression and fear.

The very next day I received some happy news about Musgo:

Today I took Mus a couple of Maltesers, because he'd said he liked them. When he saw them his face lit up and before he would take them from my hand, he went mad nuzzling me. It nearly made me cry to see that such a small thing made him so happy. He seemed so relieved that someone was listening to him and actually cared about what he wanted. He was easier to ride too. Now, whether this is because I understood him better or because he felt better about things since your visit, I don't know, but there was definitely a change in him.

Over the next few weeks I received further e-mailed updates on Musgo's progress and how he was responding to the distant Reiki sessions:

The first session I saw him sway slightly and twitch a little as though someone was massaging him. Then after about 40 minutes he came up to his door and hugged me. He appeared very chirpy and happy. The next day I rode him and he was much happier in himself. He's being braver and he's more willing to do his half-passes, which were better. He also found his extensions easier and they were better too. He has remained happier and he seems even more relaxed after his sessions. He has been very affectionate and cheeky, which is lovely to see. Everyone has noticed a difference in his ridden work, as he is calmer and more prepared to listen to me when I ask him to do his work. If he does need to run now it's not with so much violence – it's as if the urgency has gone. Quite often now he will just squeal at something and tense his muscles rather than run. I praise him for this and he keeps improving. I have found him so much easier to ride. I am doing my first competition tomorrow at the yard. It's a small one and we can just take our time if he gets stressed.

It was still less than two weeks since the communication. Musgo did brilliantly in the competition and the following week Maddi entered him in another one:

Musgo is doing so well. The healing has helped so much. He's more confident and he's straighter in his body. He always did an extended trot with his legs wide behind, but that's improved. Also, he was always bent to the right in the canter, but now he is straight.

The competition was great. During the first test he was his usual self and he wanted to run, but as I walked him out of the arena I got the overpowering feeling that the next test was going to be good. I made a fuss of him all through that test, as well as afterwards, and he was able to complete it perfectly. I was so proud of him. He tried so hard. Instead of running off, he got tense and then blew out and relaxed. I'm so pleased with him. The remedies are helping and he's really brave when he's had his 'Fears' flower essence.

Musgo was also responding really well to the confidence-boosting praise Maddi was giving him as she rode him. One day I received this news:

Mus had a big breakthrough today: he went out onto the sand arena in the sun and played! I've never seen him so happy. He looked so beautiful and it was if I could see his inner beauty shining through. I cried when he came up to me and fussed me. We seem to have a very, very strong bond now. The feeling of love and happiness I get from him now is almost overwhelming.

It was amazing that he'd improved so much over such a short period of time. I couldn't recognize the lonely, depressed and fearful horse that I'd seen in that e-mail, and he wasn't in the next one either:

He's standing with his head over the door or out of the window now. He also likes to give people a nudge and he loves playing with their zips and the Velcro on their coats. Most of all, though, he's much more relaxed when I ride him and he's completely stopped running off.

A couple of years down the line I heard from Maddi that Musgo still had the purple rug, which had remained his favourite. It never ceases to amaze me how important the colour of their rug is to horses. They are continually telling me: 'I love my rug', 'I hate this rug', 'I don't want a pink rug' or 'Can I have a royal blue one please?' The other thing that seems to upset them is having to accept a rug that has been used by a previous horse, especially a horse that has been sold on or ascended, except on the rare occasion when the new horse is proud to wear it because they recognize it has an emotional importance to their guardian or because they loved the previous horse. There are exceptions, but most horses want their own rug and they like one that reflects their personality. It's obvious when their guardian has got it right because they picture themselves wearing it so proudly.

Much later I received a heart-warming message about Musgo's inspiring transformation:

He's like a different horse now. Always calm. Quite cheeky as well, which I think is great! He's gone from being a horse that used to go into himself, almost apologizing for himself, at a competition, to a horse that has so much presence – so much that it's been commented on by judges – and is, to tell the truth, a bit of a show-off! He seems to truly love his dressage now. He loves learning new things and loves showing off what he's just learned, even when I don't really want him to. He always throws himself into whatever we are doing with seemingly never-ending energy. He always does what is asked of him and never seems to say no.

At Christmas last year we did a gala night for charity, doing dressage to music. The place was packed and he'd never done anything like it before. He was a little unsure to start with – well, for the first two seconds – and then really decided to show off. I've never felt such energy from him. He just seemed to grow. He did everything bigger and better than he had before. He was amazing.

Musgo had also won a big competition, the Music Freestyle at Medium Level, resulting in a feature with his picture in *Horse and Hound* magazine. However, it wasn't the competitions he'd won or the positive press he'd been given that touched my heart but the next e-mail:

A whole new side of Musgo has been ignited since your visit. He's developed an empathic way with others. He seems drawn to those that feel a little sad. He is the first to be with them. He literally guides people to him with his chin and holds them close to him. Everyone he's done this to says they actually feel better afterwards. He's done it to me several times and I thought it was something special between the two of us until I realized he did it for others. He seems to calm and settle people that way. He's like it with horses too. We've had two horses arrive at the yard that were quite unsettled and didn't seem happy. Musgo went to them and placed his nose on them. Within five minutes they had calmed down and we could do things with them. One has now left, a lot calmer than it arrived, and the other now lives in the stable next to Musgo and they have become great friends. Occasionally the other horse becomes nervous and Mus is the first to put his nose over the wall or through the gap to calm him. I know it sounds strange, considering how far he's come, but this is how it is. Everyone on the yard sees it too; I know I'm not imagining it.

I can't thank you enough for turning our lives around. He truly is an amazing person and it's an absolute honour to have him in my life.

Musgo's life turned full circle through one single communication, and in a way mine did too. Standing next to him, being in his presence and connecting with his energy, I discovered a feeling of trust around horses I hadn't had before. It was as if he'd given me a gift to take home that would help me with every horse I visited.

CHAPTER 9

Empowering Animals

When I first walked up the sweeping drive of the Cotswold Wildlife Park in Burford I had an epiphany that this was what animal communication was all about. What a perfect location for a workshop. I felt completeness when I thought of teaching here surrounded by wild and endangered animals. The room where I would hold the indoor part of the workshop had its own draw too: it overlooked a vista of zebra and rhino.

What I didn't realize was just how powerful this experience would be; I'd underestimated the power of the animals.

🐾 Ruby the Releaser 🐾

I wasn't dreading meeting her, but at the same time I wasn't too thrilled about it. I was feeling a stomach full of excitement twisted with a gut full of trepidation. I'd met reptiles before, but never communicated with this species – a snake who, I admit, by her very presence caused me to feel more than an inkling of fear. My other worry was about conducting this meeting, for the very first time, in front of a room full of students.

The workshop location itself was beautiful. We were sitting in the grand drawing room of a listed Victorian manor house set within 160 acres of park and gardens. There was a large marble fireplace flanked by two iron statues of parrots. On the opposite wall were three large double windows almost reaching from the ceiling to the floor, offering us a view of the rhino and zebra grazing on the grass. On the walls were gold-framed oil paintings. One of them showed a military gentleman who I was informed was Lord Tweedmouth, Reggie Heyworth's paternal great grandfather. Reggie is the current owner of the Cotswold Wildlife Park. It has been open to the public since 1970 and is home to mammals, birds, reptiles and invertebrates from all over the world.

On this cold and breezy March weekend I was holding a two-day course teaching animal communication. The attending students were after something more exciting and challenging than talking to domestic animals. This weekend they would learn to communicate with endangered animals, as well as those on the critically extinct list – animals they wouldn't naturally come in contact with. Today we would be meeting a five-foot royal python.

We didn't see her straight away. What we saw was an oblong-shaped opaque white plastic box with something dark inside. Zookeepers often call animals 'it', but I need to know a gender. The deputy of herpetology told me the snake was female; no name, though, just a number. He reassured me that she was safe to handle, but he was grinning at the same time, which caused me to wonder.

'It's OK,' he said, 'she's a teacher when schools come here for educational trips. She's used to being handled.'

Feeling more confident with the knowledge the park trusted this python with schoolchildren, I asked him to lift her out and show me the correct way to hold her. I was a true novice when it came to snakes.

The students were in awe the moment the keeper raised her out of the box. There were gasps of wonderment around the room and all eyes were on her. She was heavier than I imagined, but the most striking feeling was how leathery and smooth she felt – not slimy and repulsive at all. In fact, her skin was almost enticing, and had I been a mouse or a vole I might well have become mesmerized by her seductive quality.

As soon as I had her in my hands, it became hard to teach. I was so overwhelmed by the zillion different feelings buzzing like electrical impulses through my entire body that I remained silent for a while, just allowing the feelings to unfold. It felt as though the python was casting a magic spell on me, and within seconds I was totally enthralled by her.

I took a seat in the middle of my semi-circle of students and asked them to connect with her. While they did this, I felt that the snake was merging with me, merging her energy with mine. She could sense the ripples of fear in my hands and my legs, and no doubt through my entire body.

I presented the students with a number of questions to ask her and they fell silent as they went to work.

As they communicated with her, she and I were having our own personal experience. She was smoothly gliding her head and the front of her elongated body out of my hand and beginning to make her way up my left arm. Then she slowly moved up my white blouse towards my shoulder, her tongue darting in and out. She spoke in a mesmerizing voice, 'Let go,' she said slowly, 'let gooooo.' I took a shallow breath, held it, then breathed out and tried to relax. 'Let go,' she said once again, as she raised her head off the top of my arm and began to make her way over my chest. My body was tingling with fear now and I was concerned about where she'd go next, but I was an animal communicator and I understood better than most that she was doing 'a job' on me. She was helping me to release my fear. She was encouraging me to let it go.

'Let go,' she said again, in that voice that was seductress and human-charmer rolled into one.

She paused for a moment on my chest. My heart was thumping so hard I was surprised that everyone in the room couldn't hear it.

'Let go,' she repeated, 'let goooo.'

She now began to leave my chest and work her way over to my right arm, her tongue flicking in and out the entire time. I was trying to do as she had asked and let go of my fear. It was an illogical fear anyway. I'd never met her before, we hadn't had a horrible time together and I'd never been bitten by a snake, or confronted by one, let alone been up close and personal. There was no reason to be scared. It wasn't working, though. Despite her persistence, her slow and gentle manner, her seductive quality and charm, I still held on to some fear.

She must have felt this, because then she pushed me even further past my comfort zone. This royal python was determined to have her way. She gradually moved her body for stability and I felt her head moving up along my torso as she made her way up the centre of my chest, stretching up until her face reached the same height as my eyes. Her tongue was flicking in and out within a centimetre or two of my face. I gulped.

'Let go,' she said, her head still.

I breathed in and focused hard on letting go when I breathed out, but all I could think was *I hope she doesn't bite me*, at the same time picturing that very thing happening in my mind – the worst thing I could do.

'Let go,' she repeated, remaining in the same position, very close to my face.

I was in my own little world with her. It was as though the rest of the room had faded away.

'Let gooo,' she said slowly, this time with a gentle force in her voice, 'let go.'

At last it happened: I moved past my fear and was able to sense her properly for the first time. I felt a very emotional creature who was loving, generous and proud. The final ripples of fear left my body and I was able to sit and feel the honour of being in her presence – the honour of holding her and being this close.

My awareness came back into the room and the python came to rest in a comfy coiled position on my lap. I was now able to continue with the teaching.

I asked the students, 'How does she feel?'

'Expectant,' said one.

'As if she's about to let go of something,' said another.

'She's getting ready to move into a new period,' said the third.

'She says she's very happy because something's going to change now,' said another student.

What I had felt, after her equivalent of a therapy session with me, was a gap between her skin and herself. She pictured a space there and I got a sense of fluidity.

When I asked the keeper, he said, 'She's about to shed her skin. You can tell because her eyes are cloudy white.'

Of course, he knew that, but us novice snake lovers hadn't got a clue yet our answers still made sense.

'What does she think of her enclosure?' I put to them.

'She feels very cramped at the moment.'

'She's not happy. She wants something more interesting to look at, like branches.'

'She says it's too small.'

In fact everyone came out with a similar answer: it was too small and not interesting enough. So we were all surprised when the keeper said she only needed a very small space and wasn't interested in branches.

'There's no point giving her a large space because she won't use it. Pythons like a small place and they just coil up and sleep most of the time,' he said.

Many faces were not convinced, but out of respect I moved on to the next question. 'What does she like to eat?' I said.

'Mice,' came the first answer and then most of the room agreed.

'Chicks,' one man said and a number of people agreed with him too.

The consensus was that the mice and chicks were her preferred food, and the keeper was able to confirm that she was a fan of day-old chicks and mice when he could get them.

I wondered whether she'd like a name rather than the number which is given to each animal belonging to a large collection.

Everyone's answer was 'Yes.'

I went round one at a time, listening to what they'd picked up: 'Diamond', 'Her Highness', 'Princess', 'Sapphire', 'Garnet', 'Crystal', 'Ruby.' Each answer seemed to reflect a royal energy or a crystal energy. One student and I received the same answer: 'Ruby.' So that's what we named her. I'm sure it didn't stick. Old habits are hard to break, and there is animal husbandry etiquette, but she'd always be Ruby to us. She seemed very happy with the naming ceremony and exuded a peaceful energy.

Once I'd gone through every question and listened to the students' answers, the keeper allowed us to spend some time with Ruby. Those, like me, who had been scared at the beginning of the session had been released from their fear and could now see the real sentient being underneath the skin. With a better understanding, everyone was now keen to touch her, stroke her and give thanks. She wasn't just a teacher for schoolchildren; it came to our awareness that she was an ambassador for her species, removing the negativity and fear aimed at her kind and replacing them with stillness and love. She was passed from one pair of hands to another, photos were taken and everyone expressed how great it was to meet her.

The next day we went outside to talk to the Asiatic lion and lioness, which was another highlight of the weekend, yet many remained loyal to Ruby and the gift she had given them.

One year later I held another workshop at the Cotswold Wildlife Park and this time the head of herpetology was able to join us. Luck would have it that the scheduled snake wasn't able to come and we were blessed to have our teacher back with us again.

This time there were two people in the room who were terrified of snakes. Once we'd gone through the questions and answers, those that wanted to were allowed to hold the royal python on their lap. Most people didn't want to let her go and eked out extra time before passing her gently to the next person. One woman wasn't able to hold her, so she was passed to the next in the row. Very near the end of the semi-circle of students we reached a woman who was also very scared, but she was determined to try to get over her fear. She asked for Ruby to be placed gently on her lap, where she coiled up and closed her eyes. I rested one hand on Ruby so we were touching her together and put my other hand on the woman's back to reassure her. Tears poured down her face and onto her blouse as she appeared to experience something very personal. No words were spoken. After a few minutes her experience became too overwhelming and she asked for Ruby to be removed. Some animals have such a powerful effect on us.

The next week I received an e-mail from this student telling me she was still processing everything that had happened with Ruby. She felt the experience was so huge that there could be healing on a cellular level, something that couldn't be explained through words.

These students, just like the previous ones, were enthralled by their connection with a python and the positive effect they experienced. It was almost as though we all shed an old skin ourselves, transforming into someone more positive and accepting of a species we hadn't understood before.

Some believe that snakes possess not only the ability to poison but also the ability to heal. They represent *kundalini*, the energy of consciousness, climbing up the spine and through the energetic centres of the body. *Kundalini* is Sanskrit for 'snake' or 'serpent power'. Snake healing has been linked with inner transformation. Also, there is a medical symbol that most of us will recognize even if we don't know its name – the caduceus. It's the image of two snakes entwined round a staff. In Edward Tick's book, *The Practice of Dream Healing*, he writes, 'Some ancient sources say that the bite of one of these snakes is poisonous and the bite of the other is healing.'

In ancient Indian symbolic tradition, snakes also play an important role as guardians of the treasures of the Earth.

Whatever the belief, we all agreed there was something very magical about our snake meeting, something beyond our conscious experience. Something appeared to have happened. At the start of the session we were fearful or nervous and by the end we were smiling, laughing and stroking our newfound friend. Many of us had fallen in love, fallen under her spell. Beyond any rational explanation, we hadn't charmed the snake, the snake had charmed us.

❧ Lion Hearted ❧

On the first workshop, in the afternoon I took the students outside and we walked over to the far side of the park. We were able to see the two Asian lions through a reinforced viewing window, Chandra the male and Akela his lioness. These big cats have shaggy, tawny-coloured coats, a distinctive fold of skin that runs down the length of their belly and long tails with a black tuft at the end. Chandra was larger and more robust looking than Akela, measuring about nine feet long and roughly four feet tall, with ears protruding from a short, sandy mane that was sparser than that of his African brother. Without the heavy mane, Akela was built for speed and agility, which would be advantageous in hunting, although at the park she enjoyed waiter service. Their enclosure was oblong shaped with rolling mounds and a wooden two-level big cat climbing frame in the centre, which they could lie under in the shade, or on top of in the sun, or use as their own viewing platform.

As we arrived, Chandra and Akela were lying down behind the wire fencing over to the right side. Akela was closer to us and her regal-looking companion, Chandra, was behind her. Both had awesome-sized heads and paws. They looked relaxed and blissful in each other's company.

I'd connected with Chandra the previous afternoon to introduce myself and to check that both he and Akela would be willing to communicate. I had been immediately struck by his presence. I had also been struck by how quiet Akela seemed. When I'd connected with her I'd felt a heavy sadness cloak me. I knew her previous companion had tragically died at the end of the previous year, but I hadn't appreciated the depth of grief I'd feel from her now, four months later.

This afternoon the students were being given a unique opportunity to communicate with the 'King of the Beasts'. I started by connecting with Chandra. In one effortless movement he lifted his large majestic head and turned to look at me. His penetrating eyes seemed to look straight through me. I held my breath and remained frozen. Time seemed to stop. Even my breath seemed to stop.

This moment was broken by the screams of children and the loud conversations of their parents, who suddenly had us surrounded. They moved in between the students and began to bang on the glass to get the lions' attention. Chandra took one look in their direction then turned his head away. I sensed him disengage and felt he wouldn't communicate.

We waited patiently. Within moments the general public had grown bored and walked away. Once it was quiet we all reached out to Chandra with our loving intent and he turned his head to look back at us. He was engaging with us again.

I instructed the students, 'Reach out to Akela and see how she is feeling.'

For a moment there was silence, then I could see some of the students were visibly moved.

'What are you feeling?' I said.

'I feel a lot of sadness,' said one lady.

'I think she's upset,' said another.

A third said, 'It's like she's depressed.'

As well as feeling the depth of Akela's loss, they might, I thought, be finding that her sadness was tapping into their own feelings of loss and grief, bringing those emotions back up to the surface.

Most people didn't understand why Akela would be grieving when she had such a devoted mate lying by her side.

'She recently lost another mate,' I explained. 'Chandra is a fairly new companion. Before Chandra, she was with a lion called Sabu, who sadly got sick and died last winter. They'd been together for years.'

I was told by one of the keepers that Sabu had contracted a rare pox-like virus. There was nothing that could be done to save him and the park was left with taking the heartbreaking decision to end his suffering.

We all agreed that Akela was in a private grieving place deep down within herself where she couldn't be reached. I asked everyone to pull their connection back from her and to turn their attention to Chandra instead.

The moment I connected with him, he instructed, 'Through me,' in a deep, authoritative tone, and with it he got up. He walked with slow ease, placing each giant paw down deliberately, with power emanating from him, until he reached the near side of Akela and then lay down in front of her, blocking her from our view. He was very assertive and clear, both in his communication and in his actions.

'Chandra has said he'd like everyone to communicate with him,' I shared with the group. 'He wants us to leave Akela alone.'

We started in the usual way with questions that could be verified, but I got the feeling that Chandra was being dismissive; he didn't want to answer these questions. When I asked him whether he was happy with the size of his enclosure, his reaction caused me to want to let out a huge sigh. He wasn't interested in talking about practical things. He didn't want to talk about the size of his home or what he ate for dinner. I suggested to the students that we asked him what was important to him.

'Look at what you are doing to the Earth,' Chandra replied in a measured, powerful tone, his large face and piercing eyes now looking directly at us. 'Look at the destruction. We cannot continue like this. We have to live in harmony. You need to stop now. Start listening to us. We can live in harmony.'

I gave the students a few minutes longer and then I began to ask what they'd received.

'He thinks living in peace is important,' one of them replied.

'I felt a sense of peace,' another answered.

'I saw an image of people and animals together and felt happy,' said a third person.

'We'll ask him one more question,' I told the group, 'then once he's answered it, thank him for teaching us and sharing his knowledge and end the communication by surrounding him and Akela in your love and dissolving the connection. OK, ask him if he has a message for mankind.'

One of my students, John Greig, later read out the message he'd received in reply to this:

> No matter how the letters are rearranged in the word 'mankind', your feeling of superiority over one another is the cause of divisions between people and countries. It is only with the soul's true awakening to its spiritual intention on this Earth that you will really move forward in harmony and achieve the salvation of not only our species but the whole animal kingdom.

'Wow, that's a big message,' I said, and then I asked him to repeat it so we could all hear it again.

I think there are two ways to react to big messages like this one. We can turn them outwards and expect others to make positive changes, blaming everyone else for things that are wrong while we continue to keep our heart closed, or we can bring the messages inside ourselves for reflection so we can see how relevant they are on a personal level. Then we can act on that reflection and begin to be the change and the beacon of light that guides others by example.

Lions like Chandra and Akela are classified as critically endangered. Their entire species was nearly squeezed out of existence and now there are only about 350 remaining in the wild. I could see their enclosure at the wildlife park was a far cry from their natural existence in India's Gir Forest, but animal parks that take part in breeding programmes are essential to their continuation. We could help them in two ways: we could support projects that protect endangered animals, or we could choose to really hear the animals themselves, taking the message from their hearts into our heart by acting compassionately towards all living beings. Wouldn't that be something to be proud of?

🐾 *Aldabra Tortoises* 🐾

The following day there was strange weather, with the rain showering on and off through breaking sunshine and pelting hail. My students and I were standing exposed to the elements in front of a window separating us from the most gigantic tortoises we had ever seen. The largest would have taken about six men to move. These armoured reptiles each had a high-domed shell, a long grey neck, stocky scaled legs and enough strength to push over a small tree to munch on the tasty leaves. They were Aldabra Giant tortoises. In the morning they'd been sunning themselves and eating through the food thrown into their grassy treeless enclosure, but now they were inside their shed shelter dozing together in a huddle.

Looking at them was like looking into the face of a dinosaur. I sensed prehistoric knowledge when I looked into their beady black eyes and also a gentle quality. There was something 'otherworldly' about them that was impossible to pinpoint – maybe because it is believed that these tortoises are the longest lived of all animals.

During my lunch hour I'd had a short communication with one of the tortoises. I explained I was at the park to teach animal communication and he said, 'I know.' He said the tortoises would like to communicate with the group and I agreed to bring them across in the afternoon.

'What would you like to be asked?' I said.

This old soul replied in a deep and measured voice, 'Ask me about humanity.'

'What do you want to say about humanity?' I said.

'Life is circular. Live a slow life,' he replied.

Once we'd finished the afternoon tea break and wrapped ourselves up in coats and scarves, I led the students over to the giant tortoises. With the choice of half a dozen or so tortoises, the students were communicating with the one they felt most drawn to, the one that connected with them on a heart level. I asked them to open their connection with the tortoises and ask various questions to kick-start the communication. They were able to sense for themselves the wisdom the tortoises encompassed, a wisdom that came with years of life experience. The tortoises could live well over 100 years and even reach 150 years plus. They also had knowledge passed down from generation to generation and held energetically as a group consciousness.

Once the students had asked a number of questions, I prompted them to ask the question given by the tortoise during our lunchtime chat: 'Can you now ask them whether they have a message for humanity?'

Even though different people were asking different tortoises the question, many of them received the same kind of response: 'Slow down', 'Live life at a slower pace', 'Slow down and live every moment', 'Stop rushing' and 'Take life more slowly.'

It seems obvious that a tortoise would communicate something about slowing down or moving more slowly – after all, that's what they do. But I think sometimes animals do communicate something that appears obvious and simple, based upon what they know. They draw on their own life experience and how they see the world, just like human animals do. The hardest thing for us is to listen to that good advice and then apply it to our everyday lives.

One of my students, Babette Tegldal, told me she'd received this message from a tortoise:

The tortoises struggle to understand humans, as mankind on the whole refuses to connect with the 'energy' – the energy of the Earth – and in consequence our own energies are out of balance. They wish we would slow down, find some equilibrium, which would allow us to focus better. They almost hold us in contempt, as these are very simple skills to them, yet we struggle with the 'baby steps'. One tortoise in particular showed me the word 'nature' in a beautiful pictorial way, so for me personally I have to make sure I don't ignore the beauty around me, which they marvel at.

Tortoises evolved over 200 million years ago and have remained relatively unchanged over time. Maybe this is the reason why they seem such ancient wise beings. The Aldabra is the second largest species of tortoise after the Galapagos tortoise. You may have heard of the last remaining Galapagos tortoise, the infamous 'Lonesome George', aged between 90 and 100, who holds the *Guinness Book of World Records* title of 'rarest living creature'. The tortoises on the Galapagos Islands were hunted for their meat close to the point of extinction and once goats were introduced to their habitat they ate their way through it, virtually wiping the Galapagos tortoises off the planet. Darwin landed in 1835 with the crew of the *Beagle* and he ate the tortoise meat too, but later spoke of the need to protect them as a species. Luckily the Aldabra tortoises fared better and there is a colony of about 150,000 of them on the islands of the Aldabra atoll in the Seychelles, the largest population in the world.

CHAPTER 10

Balance Matters

THERE ARE SOME communications that completely blow my mind because of their intimacy and accuracy. This incredible success story is one of them.

🐾 *Darwin's Outlook* 🐾

As I pulled up on the curve of a narrow road in the heart of Battersea suburbia, the door of a house nearby opened. A handsome-looking chocolate flat-coat retriever came out to the gate, followed swiftly by a short slim middle-aged woman with medium-brown hair waving a piece of paper, which turned out to be a parking permit. I recognized the good-looking canine as Darwin and guessed the tired-faced human must be Michele, his guardian. They had been referred to me by renowned veterinary surgeon Richard Allport, who opened the Natural Medicine Centre, a referral centre for animals.

Darwin was now two-and-a-half years old, but when he was only four months he had swallowed a sock. The emergency vet had wanted to operate, but Michele hadn't been keen and the vet had suggested liquid paraffin as an alternative. After the paraffin had been administered, the sock had come through with ease, but since then Darwin had been suffering and it was thought that the treatment might have permanently damaged his stomach. He wasn't absorbing food and was always having the runs. He had grown very thin and Michele had tried all sorts of options to help him. When his troubles had been at their most severe, he had almost died.

'I have since been working with two wonderful vets, Richard Allport and Richard Bleckman,' Michele wrote to me. 'Darwin is now strong and mostly healthy, yet still on chicken and rice and when we tried a month or so ago to make the transition back to normal food, all his old symptoms came back. I have been rebuilding him since then.'

Michele went on to tell me in the beginning she couldn't sleep through a night without Darwin waking her up because he needed a fast trip to the garden, where he'd suffer chronic diarrhoea. For a year and a half he was very sick and Michele suffered sleep deprivation. It grew so bad the situation was affecting her health and she was in danger of losing her privately run business and even her home. Others would have caved in at that point, but Michele's bond with Darwin was strong and she wasn't prepared to give up on him. Her belief was that once you take on a pet they are your responsibility. I was reminded of the words of Charles Darwin: 'A man's friendships are one of the best measures of his worth.' Thankfully over the past year, with the assistance and knowledge of the two highly distinguished vets, things had improved and Darwin's attacks of diarrhoea were now more sporadic than constant.

'I believe there is an emotional or mental pattern which contributes to his flare-ups and I am keen to explore every avenue to help heal him,' Michele continued in her e-mail. 'He is very sociable and has tons of mates on Clapham Common and beyond. He is great with children and patient. He has great dog sitters who adore him and he them, as I run my own business and am out at meetings two or three times a week. So would you like to meet us and see what we can achieve?'

I greeted both of them at the gate and was met by two joyful smiles. Darwin met me like an old friend, without the necessity of a sniff, and when I introduced myself as the lady he'd spoken to earlier in the week he replied, 'I know.'

We positioned ourselves in the living room and I took out the notepad on which I'd written down our distant communication. Darwin remained close by my feet for most of the consultation, checking I would repeat everything he'd said without bottling out and being on hand to reply to any questions Michele might want to ask. He was being the model client, supporting both his guardian and his go-between communicator.

I began by running through the first impressions I'd received from him, including some of the details I'd already e-mailed to Michele for verification.

'Darwin comes across as a happy-go-lucky, easy-going dog. He pulls on the lead, loves sniffs and loves bounding,' I repeated.

'Yes, all those things are Darwin,' she said.

'I feel he is very affectionate, he loves people and life, he loves playing with a red ball and has a blanket in the living-room.'

'His lavender blanket is normally on the sofa and the red ball is his friend's ball but he loves to play with it,' said Michele.

'He's so happy to be alive, thrilled in fact, and treats each day as a blessing. He pictured the lining of his stomach as porous, holey, from damage, and said acidity ate away at the lining.'

'That's what the vet said. In fact, that same word, "porous",' Michele replied.

'The other things he expressed were that his stomach was sore. He mentioned an acid/alkaline imbalance and said the good bacteria couldn't cope. He also said he was all right, though, and you worried too much. He said you were hanging on to the fear.'

I didn't know what fear Darwin was talking about, but it appeared to mean something to Michele, who looked at me and then at Darwin. 'He told you that?' she said, surprised and concerned.

This was Michele's first experience of receiving a communication with an animal and I could imagine her thought patterns struggling to cope. It wasn't that she was close-minded; I felt she was just starting to comprehend how clear Darwin could be. But this was just the beginning and he was warming her up gently. He had much bigger news to impart. But for now I continued with his initial communication.

'I asked him whether he'd been given any vitamin E to help him recover from the sock incident and he said, "No,"' I told Michele.

'That's right. They didn't give him anything,' she confirmed.

'I asked him why he'd swallowed the sock and he said it was to blanket the discomfort. I checked this by asking him if it was an accident and he said, "No, definitely not. My tummy hurt."'

'That could be right,' Michele said. 'At four months old he was being fed adult food rather than puppy food and he might have had tummy ache. It was an awful mistake. My friend went to pick it up from a cash and carry and neither of us realized he should be on puppy food still.'

'He says his kidneys are sore because they're working hard to remove toxins,' I said.

'He's been prescribed pancreatic enzymes to help with that.'

'I also checked whether this was something to do with his birth and his mother. He said that she was a good mother; she licked him and was very proud. He showed himself playing with his brothers and sisters, being inquisitive and bright, joining in and sleeping with them. Nothing was wrong then and his tummy was fine.'

'I had been wondering whether it was a genetic problem,' said Michele.

'I asked him whether you went to collect him as a puppy on your own and he gave me the impression you went with your husband or partner but said you were now separated.'

Michele told me she had planned to pick up Darwin with her partner but he had kept making excuses. Darwin had already told me they'd been having problems; it had been about the time that he'd arrived that the relationship had come to an end. He said he worried about Michele, not himself, felt very responsible for her and loved her a lot.

'We have an intense relationship,' he told me. 'She has felt very low. She doesn't want to go there again. She had health problems. Now she is very strong, but she worries.'

I felt I needed to ask him, 'What sort of health concerns?'

'Tiredness, blocked energy, weight gain, being unable to socialize,' he replied.

Michele was moved by Darwin's comprehension of her feelings, which she'd tried her best to hide, and quietly began to cry.

'Are you OK?' I said.

'I feel sad that my lack of well-being concerns him so much,' she replied.

While amazed Darwin was aware of these things, she agreed with them. She said she had been withdrawing, staying in as much as possible, that she'd also had severe back pain and, to top it off, had become a chocolate addict – she just couldn't stop herself – but she was better than she had been.

I returned to the subject of Darwin's stomach and digestion and asked him how the liquid paraffin had affected him.

'It spread, killing everything. Red blood cells transmuted. White blood cells went into fierce attack,' he said.

'Transmuted?' quizzed Michele. 'That's the word our vet used. I can't believe Darwin knows that.'

'Darwin says every three or four weeks he has a weakness, a flare-up,' I said.

'Yes!' Michele was looking from me to Darwin and back again, totally astounded.

We'd reached the end of my third page of notes, which ended my first impressions. Now we'd move on to Michele's questions to Darwin and I would read out what Darwin had told me.

'Your first question is, "How can I lead you better?" Darwin said, "It's not a leadership issue." He is a high-energy dog who loves life, he's exuberant and interested in girls. Male dogs think he's fun. He has a slightly dominant edge, due to being intact, but he's not interested in making puppies, he's just enjoying life. He says the flare-ups are triggered by your stress. He takes it on board and because he has an area of weakness in the stomach it hits that first. I asked him to pinpoint problem areas.'

Darwin then told me something I could never have anticipated: 'Menstrual bleed.' I was wary of saying this to Michele because it was very personal and what if I was wrong? I was wondering whether to skip to the next piece of information when Darwin, who was still at my feet, spoke up. 'Say it,' he pushed. I trusted that he knew it was important and repeated his words.

Michele sat silently. I waited. She looked at me. Then she looked at Darwin. Then back at me again. 'He said that?' she said.

More silence followed and then Michele started to cry. It took a few minutes for her to compose herself before she was able to speak, but then she told me she'd been suffering terribly and had been completely wiped out by months and months of constant bleeds. She felt embarrassed that Darwin knew this and also powerless to do anything about it. This was the worst part of her health problems and was still continuing. She'd found it very hard to fight the exhaustion it brought.

She rummaged to find a box of tissues and I waited for her to gain composure before we continued.

I explained to her that Darwin had gone on to say that the stomach problems were 'locked in' and he felt she had a pain, which he also called a 'blockage', and he wanted her to remove it rather than pouring 'more cover onto it'. He also wanted to say at the time he was adopted he knew she was feeling what he called 'a huge agony, a feeling of pain and a cover-up'.

Michele told me the day she had adopted Darwin and brought him home she had been feeling very low. Her relationship was over and although she had sensed it coming, it was still a shock. That evening she had watched *Out of Africa* with Darwin snuggling into her side and cried all night.

I got the feeling Darwin was Michele's spiritual leader. 'He is bringing balance, because it matters,' I said to her. 'He is teaching you everything you need to know. Through this you will grow stronger and wiser. Through this you will help even more people. He says, "Step into your spiritual path and be enlightened." He remains joyful because he knows this is your intended journey and he will do anything for you.'

There was so much to take in from Darwin's response to this one question. We took a break and fetched some water.

Once we'd settled again we continued with Michele's second question. 'What do you need from me to heal your digestive disorder?' she'd asked.

This time Darwin was short and to the point: 'More focus, more clarity, more inner peace. You work too hard, don't play enough and where are the holidays?'

The third question was: 'What else can I do to help you relax?'

Darwin replied, 'Relax yourself. Find inner peace. I worry about *you*, always *you*.'

'Are the house and garden making you ill?' Michele asked. 'Or is it what the neighbours next door give their pigeons?' She explained to me that the pigeons came over the fence and Darwin ate them.

Darwin replied, 'Our environment is not peaceful. Need to house sweep.' He showed me a picture of negative energy coming from the back of the house through to the front. Then he pictured Michele's garden and said anger was coming into it from the right. This made sense to her because she was having an ongoing disagreement with her neighbour over a couple of issues.

Then there was a feeling that Darwin had blocked pores/cells/atoms that needed major unblocking or cleansing. It was as though a vibration had been left behind in his stomach, a feeling of paraffin on his stomach lining, which prevented nutrients from being absorbed, and then acid built up and he went into acid overload.

Michele was taking notes as we went along. Her fifth question was: 'When he is unable to digest his food without medication and special food, what is he communicating?'

'I'm feeling tired, a bit run down. I can feel your frantic energy,' Darwin explained. Then he pictured Michele and said that she would benefit from a lot of calming on a cellular level, as she was locked in as a carer. He asked, 'Where else does she pour her love?'

In her initial contact Michele had requested a consultation to see how she could be a better pack leader for Darwin. Having already spent what she described as a 'small fortune on potions and vets and medicine for him', she was looking elsewhere for answers and a resolution. As we progressed through the consultation she was hearing more and more that Darwin was advising *her* and on a whole heap of different issues, focusing on subjects he felt important and helpful.

With the next question she asked, 'What can I do as a leader to reduce his tension?'

'Take control of yourself, your own energy,' Darwin said succinctly.

In contrast, he had much more to say in answer to Michele's final question, 'What can I do or stop doing to be the best leader for him?'

'Keep calm at all times. Take control of your life and I will respect that. Don't feel sorry for me. Boost your self-esteem, then think of mine. Don't worry about me. Act as though everything is "normal". Then the vibration will "die" and all will be well.'

'He wants you to see him as healthy, happy and balanced,' I said to Michele. 'That's what matters.'

Two months later Michele contacted me again:

The last couple of months have been intense, to say the least. Yet I truly did listen. I relaxed much more with Darwin, stopped fussing and started trusting more. For his part, he has stopped waking me up in the night. It has been fantastic. His faeces have been normal bar one or two days all this time. This is a miracle.

Also realizing I needed to work less intensely, I booked a few days in the Yorkshire countryside with him as part of the 'taking a holiday' recommendation. Unfortunately my father became acutely ill, so I had to cut it short, but the three days we did have on the moors together were so very special. Darwin met goats where we were staying and bounded around the moors without a care in the world. My father is much better now, thankfully, and I am organizing his ninetieth birthday party! When I went away Darwin's 'holiday home' friends said his energy was the best they had ever seen it and it is true that he sleeps much less now. We did a 10-mile walk on Saturday that he loved and he wasn't tired the next day, which I'd expected him to be. I can only put this all down to you creating a more balanced relationship between us. Balance really does matter.

CHAPTER 11

Lucy Goosey

NOT EVERY animal I communicate with is curled up on the sofa in the safety of their home. Some go missing and their guardians contact me to locate them. This is the most advanced aspect of an animal communicator's responsibilities, as it incorporates the skills of both body gestalt (moving your consciousness inside the animal to sense how they feel) and remote viewing (viewing distant locations), but is simply called 'tracking'. I'm going to share with you one of my most unusual tracking cases.

It had been a hard few weeks, let alone days. I was exhausted and needed to rest, but then late in the evening the telephone rang. I was just debating whether to run down the hall to answer it or crawl up to bed when I recognized the voice of Beth, one of my workshop organizers, sounding distressed. She was in the middle of leaving a message when I picked up the phone and said, 'Are you all right? What's the matter?'

'We've got a bit of a crisis here. Lucy is missing!' she said.

'Oh no,' I said. I'd fallen in love with this opinionated goose when she'd been the star teacher at my workshop in Bath only two weeks earlier. 'Tell me what happened.'

'She got out this afternoon and the last we saw of her she was heading across the wooden bridge close to the house. We've been looking for hours but we can't find her, and now it's getting dark and I don't know where she is. If she's got into one of the streams or rivers around here she could be in the Bristol Channel by now, as they all head to the sea and the current can be really strong. I just wondered whether you could say if she's still alive.'

As Beth was speaking I was already honing my connection with Lucy. Luckily, we'd formed an energetic link at the workshop, so all I had to do was recall her image in my mind and reach out to her with love. She immediately hooked into my frequency and began to communicate.

'She's picturing herself going out of a gate, then out of the front and turning left. Is that correct?' I said to Beth.

'Yes, it is. She went out of the front of the house and we know she turned left. Can she tell you where she is? Is she still alive?' Beth had a note of panic in her voice. 'It's dark and there are so many foxes here. If they come across her – well, I don't think she'd survive the night. I'm sure they'd kill her.'

'Tell her I'm all right,' were Lucy's first words to me. She was keen to reassure Beth.

I relayed the message and then felt a wave of anger from Lucy. 'She's very angry, though,' I said.

'Why?'

'I'm not sure, I just feel anger. Maybe it's because she's not where she wants to be? The main thing is she is alive, so keep searching for her.'

'Thank God for that. It's getting dark now, but I'll go out for as long as I can. What if I don't find her?' Beth replied.

'You need to remain calm, OK? I know it's hard, but it will help support her if you're calm. Remember she can connect with everything you're feeling. I can't do anymore now, I've got a terrible headache. You know how draining this work can be. But I can help you properly tomorrow.'

'You do sound awful. Thank you for telling me that much, it helps a lot. It's just so nice to know she's still alive and we haven't been searching for hours in vain.'

'E-mail me tomorrow and let me know what's happening. If she's not home by 5 p.m., I'll communicate with her again and call you.'

'OK. Thanks, Pea,' said Beth.

At 8 a.m. the next day, I communicated with Lucy again. I couldn't wait all day to try and help them both. We had a very quick communication and I sent Beth an e-mail:

I picture her hiding under something low to the ground. When I get back in late this afternoon let me know if you've still not found her and I'll communicate with her again. One more thing just came to me – she's fairly close to your house, on the same side. It's as if she feels trapped. She wants to see you.

Just before I ran out of the door to a day full of appointments
I read Beth's response:

> Bless you, bless you, Pea, for trying – I could hear from your voice
> how drained you were yesterday, but your news that she was alive
> kept me from suffering her loss last night. Tried hard, as you can
> imagine, visualizing her, but no luck as yet. Have been out since
> 6 a.m. looking and calling to her. Very odd that she is not respond-
> ing to my voice, as she always does. If she can only call and keep
> calling, I can track her down so easily. Have dropped reward notes
> into every building in the lane and my husband has asked all the
> staff at school to keep an eye out for her, so as long as she has not
> been taken by someone for the pot, we should find her. I just need
> her to call out to me. Thanks for still thinking of her. I'm off out
> now to look again ...

When I got in I checked my e-mails, but it wasn't good news:

> Still no sign, very sadly. If she is still alive, *please* ask her to call
> loudly and repeatedly when she hears me calling her.

I immediately delved through a pile of papers to retrieve Lucy's
photo then reached out to connect with her. It only took a
second before my opinionated goose friend was telling me
what to do.

'I'm all right. Tell her I'm all right,' she told me in no uncer-
tain terms.

'Good, I'm glad you're OK. Now, where are you?' I said.

'Not far away. Look under the shelter.'

'Under the shelter?' I'd been to Lucy and Beth's home and roughly knew the area but didn't know where she was talking about.

'*The shelter!*' she shouted in a way that seemed to say Beth or I should know what she was talking about. It was as though she was saying, 'The shelter, it's obvious! Oh, come on, the *shelter!*'

I didn't manage to talk to Beth until about 8 p.m., when the light was slowly beginning to fade and she returned home. I repeated what Lucy had told me, but Beth didn't know where she meant. She was shattered, she'd been awake all night worrying, and said she and her neighbour had kept their windows open, even though it was very cold, just in case they could hear Lucy calling.

'I've been out all day with lots of my neighbours and we haven't seen or heard her,' she said. 'I'm so worried about her being out there another night. For all I know someone might pick her up and have her for dinner. No one's going to suspect that she's a family pet.'

I tried to tune out of Beth's fears and anxiety so they wouldn't distract me from my connection with Lucy, but it wasn't easy, as she was preparing herself for the worst.

'I just need to know one way or the other,' she said point blank.

I reconnected with Lucy. 'What does the shelter look like?' I asked her. For a split-second I got an image of a bus stop, but then my logical mind kicked in and dismissed it. I knew

Beth and Lucy lived down a quiet country lane surrounded by picturesque fields and fox burrows.

'At the bottom of the shelter,' said Lucy and she pictured a steep bank. At the bottom of the bank I could see a source of water large enough to be a river. The way she showed the bank it looked as though there was about a six-foot drop from the top of it to the water below. 'You're looking in the wrong direction,' she added.

She went on to picture her legs wrapped in twine or something similar and I had the feeling that she was trapped, unable to move. I finished my report with, 'She can't get out, Beth. She's feeling trapped and I think she might be caught up in some twine. She's also feeling cold.'

'At least she might remain in the same spot then,' said Beth, 'I can think of two places where she might be. One is a steep bank across the field that has a river leading into the Bristol Channel and the other is round to the back of me.'

'She's picturing big leaves, a bit like oversized ivy leaves. They're dark green and by the water,' I relayed.

'Can't move,' said Lucy, picturing the bank again.

'Obviously there's too much of a climb for her to get out,' I said to Beth.

'Do you want to get back?' I asked Lucy. I wanted to check that she hadn't gone because she'd had enough.

'Yes. Of course. Stupid question,' she said, making it very clear.

One of Beth's concerns, which I shared, was that Lucy might have left because she'd achieved what she'd come to do

– she'd taught that geese can communicate their feelings and that they have very strong opinions. So I had to check: 'Have you gone because you've finished teaching?'

'No, it's my home and I want to be there,' she replied.

'How far away are you?'

'One mile.'

That was all the information Beth needed. With the two places in mind, she got on the phone to her neighbour. They each took a location; Beth took the one furthest away across the field.

When I was off the phone, I asked Lucy one more question: 'Will we find you?'

'Yes,' came the answer.

I don't know how animals can answer this question, but they often do. They seem to have a knowing about things totally beyond any logical reasoning.

Forty-five minutes later, the phone rang.

'We've found her! She's home!' screamed Beth, totally over-joyed.

'Where was she?' I said, smiling and relieved.

'My neighbour found her. She went out with her dog, Daisie, and they got to a grass verge and Daisie just started barking. She was facing a bank with a deep drop – literally pointing her nose towards the bank – and she wouldn't let up.'

'Was she pointing towards Lucy?' I said.

'Yes! When my friend reached the bank she couldn't see anything until she leaned all the way out. Then she could see Lucy tucked into the bank below. Daisie was barking and Lucy was honking back to her. Daisie actually jumped down to Lucy, but instead of the game she normally plays, chasing Lucy around the garden, she stood totally still, just looking at her, as if she knew Lucy was upset and she was being company for her.'

'I am so thrilled, I can't tell you,' I said.

'I'm ecstatic! I can't believe she's home!' cried Beth.

'So where did the shelter come into this?'

'Well, that was just genius. The bank is on the edge of a large car park and directly below a large white derelict bus.'

'You're kidding? One of the pictures she gave me was of a bus stop, but I dismissed it. So there *was* literally a bus that had stopped. A bus stop!'

'That's right, a stopped bus. It never moves,' said Beth.

'Well, that will teach me a lesson. I must remember never ever to dismiss a detail, however bizarre it sounds, even when I think it doesn't fit. She was giving us a clue.'

I was thankful we'd got to Lucy in time. I loved her forthright attitude, protective nature and aristocratic air. At the workshop she had literally held court; we had all sat in a semicircle around her and when she'd answered a few questions and could see she had our full attention she had relaxed and sat down directly in the centre at the front to answer the rest, possibly the happiest goose on the planet.

CHAPTER 12

The Well-Mannered Guest

THERE ARE SOME animals who are quite simply members of our family. For them life is about one thing – companionship. Thornton Wilder, an American playwright and novelist, once said, 'We can only be said to be alive in those moments when our hearts are conscious of our treasures.' Jack has always been one such treasure.

❧ *Jack* ❧

Jack – such an ordinary kind of name, but this Jack was named after extraordinary circumstances. You see, he got his name from his predecessor and to understand his importance to his guardians, Christine and her husband Paul, I need to tell you a story.

In the very beginning Christine and Paul lived in a faraway land in a city called Muscat, the capital of a beautiful country called the Sultanate of Oman. The other member of their family was a stunning black stray oriental kitten called Sooty, who had adopted them.

One day after a freak rain shower Christine was parking her car outside her home when she noticed a Jack Russell-type dog gingerly making his way towards her. She approached him and he immediately ran back to a sodden cardboard box left abandoned on wasteland close to her house. As she got closer she saw it was punctured with holes and inside there was a blanket and a couple of tins of dog food. She deduced someone must have dumped the dog in the hope that she and Paul would take him in. But it wasn't that simple. They weren't in a position to adopt a puppy, as they were literally about to leave Oman for good.

They took their little Jack-in-the-Box into their home and fed him, then tried to find him a permanent residence. It turned out Little Jack was an adventurous guy and liked to go on field trips out of Sooty's puppy-sized catflap, often to be rescued from the busy road out front. After advertising and numerous attempts to rehome him with families who always returned him, Christine and Paul felt left with only two options: 1. take him to Scotland; 2. have him put to sleep. Having already stretched their resources by committing to bringing Sooty back with them, after much agonizing they felt they had no choice. They couldn't bear what they were about to do, but also couldn't bear the thought of Little Jack dying from heat exhaustion and starvation, feeling sad and unloved, on the streets of a country not renowned for its love of animals.

It was the most excruciating decision of their lives. On the day the vet was due to visit, Christine couldn't bear to stay at home and went to see a friend. Paul took Jack in their battered open jeep to the driving range and vented his frustration on a bucket of golf balls. He'd tied Jack's collar to the frame of the jeep with a piece of rope, but when he returned 30 minutes later he found the rope had come loose. Nevertheless, Jack had decided to stay on the passenger seat watching him.

Back at the house the local vet arrived, one of only two in the country, the chemicals were administered and Jack slipped away. This was the first time that Paul had experienced anything like this and he was surprised by how upset he felt. For years afterwards, both Paul and Christine regretted having to make that decision, and the story could end here with feelings of overwhelming frustration, pain and a mountain of guilt, but thankfully it doesn't.

Back in Scotland, Christine and Paul visited Sooty three times a week while he sat out his prison sentence behind bars in quarantine. When he emerged six months later he saw a frozen white landscape he could never have imagined while in the Middle East. However, the snow wasn't to be his only surprise.

Just before Sooty came home Paul's brother and sister-in-law were expecting puppies from their black Labrador. With both parents and all four grandparents being black, it was assumed that a litter of little black faces would appear, but to everyone's utter disbelief, the firstborn was a golden male – a fawn-coloured Andrex puppy. After their brief relationship with Little Jack of Oman and the agony of their decision, there was no question in Christine's mind that the golden bundle of joy in front of her would become the newest member of their family. He would be called Jack, in honour of Jack-in-the-Box. That day it seemed as if the sunshine was pouring out of his golden face.

Sooty wasn't so pleased and didn't take to Jack at first – the lively puppy put his nose out of joint – but with a couple of choice swipes, the hierarchy was soon established.

It was a cool November day in 2006 when I was first introduced to Jack by an e-mail from Christine. She and Paul had now moved to Wales and she had read a book called *Animals and the Afterlife* by Kim Sheridan, which referred to animal communicators. Up to that point Christine and Paul had never even heard of animal communication.

When I clicked on the photo attached to Christine's e-mail, I saw a happy-faced dog lying on the grass gazing lovingly towards something out of shot. He was clearly an adult and Christine informed me the firstborn golden boy was now eight years old. The thought of communicating with Jack and Sooty sounded exciting to Christine, so she had made contact to request sessions with both of them. Paul, on the other hand, was not convinced. Years after the consultations he told me he'd been impressed by the clairvoyants he'd visited and their intuition or perception or whatever it was, but the thought of communicating with animals in a language that we could interpret seemed a bit too far-fetched to him.

The moment I connected with Jack I came across a gentleman. He was also completely adorable, the kind of animal you want to throw your arms around to give them a big hug. Jack was absolutely the huggable type – happy and exuding a joy for life. He shared one of his happy deep barks.

'What do you like to play with?' I asked him.

Jack returned an image of a ball and I felt his excitement.

'Have you got any favourite foods? Is there anything you adore?'

He was even more excited by the thought of food and I saw what I thought must be a bowl of chicken. Following this I saw dry food and felt tenderness in my own stomach.

'How do you feel after dry food?' I prompted.

Jack pictured the wet food again and the soreness in my stomach stopped.

'OK, Jack, so you've got a delicate stomach and you prefer the wet food to the dry,' I confirmed with him.

Jack and I continued to exchange information using the senses. I asked him questions and he answered them. I received an image, or a sensation, or sometimes just a knowing. I wrote all the impressions down so I could e-mail them to Christine:

He spends most of his time with you because your husband is away a lot. His sight is cloudy. His rear teeth are slightly decayed. He needs some bones or tripe to chew on. No more bread – he feels stodgy. He could be a bit fitter; he'd benefit from more exercise. He loves walking by the sea. And finally, he comes across as very strong, but gentle. He's not pushy. He loves Sooty, but he doesn't think that Sooty is so fond of him.

Christine wrote back:

> It sounds like my Jack. His favourite toy is a ball. He loves chicken.
> In fact, we have to be careful what we give him because he has
> had a lot of stomach problems, mainly diarrhoea. He can't eat rich
> food and hates dry food. My husband is away a lot and Jack's sight
> is a problem. He adores walking by the sea. It's his favourite place.
> As soon as we near the beach, he's almost hyperventilating
> because he's so excited. And you're right, he is very strong, but he's
> not pushy, he's really a gentle teddy bear. I think he'd like to be
> closer to Sooty, but Soots keeps his distance.

Both Christine and I felt happy that we had Jack on the line,
so to speak, so we continued with the communication and I
began to ask Jack Christine's questions.

'Christine wants to ask you whether you are happy with her
and Paul?'

'Very, very happy. I love life,' Jack replied with feeling of joy
bubbling over like freshly poured champagne.

'Do you feel well, Jack?'

I felt stiffness in my own hips and lack-lustre energy.
Combined, this would make it hard for Jack to move and I
could sense he'd like more energy because he loved his walks.

'Christine would like to know why you don't like getting into
the car,' I said to him.

'I feel sick, my balance is not good and I find it scary. They
let me sit in the rear, but that doesn't help. It makes me feel
ill,' he replied.

I could feel he only got in the car because he was asked. I wondered whether his balance problems were linked to his poor sight.

'Would you like a doggie friend?' I said.

'No, I am happy as the only one,' replied Jack, 'but I would like more adventures. I sleep a lot during the day and would rather go out.'

Christine and I arranged a telephone appointment and I relayed everything Jack had expressed. He pulled on the lead, so we talked about treat training in the garden to help make it easier to take him out on the lead in public places. I felt Christine and Paul might be being a bit too soft with Jack, their first canine companion, and suggested they behave a little more positively and visualize him staying close to their side rather than pulling on the lead.

Christine wanted to ask Jack, 'Do you mind staying with our friends and their dog, Max, when we go away?'

'No, I don't mind, they are lovely, but I miss you and wish I could come too,' Jack replied.

'Is there anything you would like to tell me?' said Christine.

'I love you so much,' said Jack.

I immediately saw an image of Jack with his paws up on shoulders trying to lick a face. I could feel that he loved hugs and cuddles and being physically close. I felt he would do anything for Christine and Paul. He might appear daft sometimes, but this was because he was still a puppy at heart.

'Does he love my mum?' Christine wanted to ask.

'She's a really lovely gentle person. I really love her,' said Jack. Then he pictured an angel.

'He considers your mum to be an angel,' I told Christine. 'He says she's a very special person, gentle and centred. Both he and Sooty have bonded with her and feel very safe. Jack says she takes time to talk to them both.'

'She does. She has a very special relationship with them,' said Christine.

She had one final question: 'Are you Little Jack reincarnated?'

'No, I am myself,' replied Jack.

Christine then explained to me about Jack of Oman. As she told me about the box and the dog food and the blanket I began to sense Little Jack's presence energetically and started to receive his message for Christine.

'Little Jack comes across as wiser than Jack Senior and watches and guides you. He says you were beautiful people and it was his time to go. You helped him over. There was blackness in his chest – in fact he was very ill – and he was very unhappy. He needed you to help him and that was why he came to you. He said he was the love of your life before Jack Senior.'

For a while there was silence down the end of the phone. Christine and Paul had felt guilty over their forced decision for the past eight years. Now, for the first time, a complete stranger was telling them it was OK. The sweet little puppy that had landed metaphorically on their doorstep had seemed to be in the right place, at the right time and with the right people. As agonizing as it had been to put a seemingly healthy puppy to sleep, here was that same puppy in spirit form saying it was the right thing to do.

With a bit of a waver in her voice, Christine said, 'Can you say one more thing to our Jack? Do you know we love you?'

Jack jumped in straight away, 'Oh yes! I feel it every day. It warms my heart. I know how much.'

In February 2008 Christine requested another communication with Jack. Things had changed. Since the previous communication he had begun to bump into things and couldn't always see his ball. Christine wanted to hear what he had to say about it.

'How is your eyesight? Is it getting worse?' she asked.

'I can feel some aching behind the eyes,' I told her, 'and his sight seems dim now, rather than cloudy. Everything seems darker.'

'Are your eyes causing you any pain?' she said.

'Jack gives me the feeling his right eye aches quite a bit, but he also says he doesn't want anything done about it.'

Christine continued, 'Are you in pain with your joints?'

'His hip joints feel a little painful and the right one is worse than the left. He showed me a picture of his walk, which is a real hip-swinging kind of waddle,' I told her.

'You were squealing in pain a few weeks ago. What was hurting so much?'

'He's showing me his right forepaw. It hurts at the wrist joint. He found it hard to put it down.'

'Can he tell you why he was so reluctant to walk along a

certain section of our daily route and refused to pass a specific part of the road?' said Christine.

'Some dogs are very sensitive and Jack is one of them. He said he'd sensed bad energy and that death was coming to take someone and he didn't want it to be him. He said to trust him – he was not happy about it.'

'Why won't you go out at night for your last walk after dark?'

Jack answered, 'It's not safe.'

'He also feels it is important to be in the house,' I explained to Christine.

'Why don't you like getting into my car but don't mind getting into Paul's?' Christine said.

'I like to be with Paul and I feel a need to protect him.'

I told Christine it felt as though Jack was taking on Paul's pain in his right hip and was helping relieve it. 'He loves being close to Paul and helping him with his hip.'

'Tell him we're sorry that we've been busy and unable to take him to the beach. Can you ask whether he would like to go?'

'Yes, always,' Jack responded lightning fast, 'but as a family. It's a special walk.'

'What does he really want to do when we go out for a walk?'

Jack replied, 'Play, sniff, smell the fresh air. Just be with you. Feeling free is wonderful.'

I could sense Christine smiling down the other end of the phone. 'My mum would like to know what he is asking her when she plays ball with him in our garden. Jack puts his paws up on the bench and looks into her eyes as if he's asking her something.'

I felt a wonderful warm sensation as Jack replied, 'I'm just telling her how much I adore her and how worried I am about my family. She understands. We are very close. We have a heart connection. She is very loving and supportive of me. I love her to bits. We often feel the same – protective and a little achy.'

'Pea, do you feel there is anything we can do to make him more comfortable? Happier? Pain-free?'

'Jack is suggesting massaging his hips, just like Paul has a massage. He's also requesting more lovely cuddles on the sofa. More lovely chicken, or mackerel, or sardines in tomato sauce,' I said, smiling.

Christine laughed and said she'd see what she could do.

'Is there anything you want to tell us? Or feel we should know?' she added.

It always amazes me how the most important question is inevitably the one where the guardian asks if there is anything the animal would like to say, actually giving them a blank page to express their thoughts or feelings.

'Jack has said a number of things,' I began to prepare Christine, 'and they may not be what you're expecting.' I then relayed what Jack had said, word for word: 'Even though my time might not be long I have loved every minute of "being" and I love you both. My life has been so special and I have *no* regrets. Whenever it is my time I will go peacefully and with a grateful heart because I have felt so loved and adored. *You are my everything – everything to me, forever more*.'

'Please know we love you very much,' Christine said out loud to him.

'I know, Mummy, I feel it,' he replied, and I repeated it out loud for her.

In January 2009 Christine requested another communication with Jack. I communicated with him through his photo again and once more gave space for him to express himself before I began with Christine's questions.

Once I connected with Jack I immediately felt he was sad, sore and exhausted. I could also tell he was having difficulty breathing. I saw an image of him walking slowly and stiffly. When I used a technique to look out of his eyes I could tell his sight was worse – it was now quite dark. I felt his painful wrists, as my own wrists ached, and heard the sound of noisy breathing as he pictured sleeping at night. I could sense he was sleeping a lot, he felt weary and I had an urge to give him a big cuddle. There was sadness in his eyes that had the effect of cloaking me in sadness. He told me he was trying to get excited about walks, especially for 'Daddy'. It was hard not to feel emotional when he expressed how much he adored both Christine and Paul and worshipped his hero, Sooty. Despite his physical discomfort and sadness, he was still able to show how much he loved his family. In this moment, where he was free to express whatever he wished, I sensed he knew he was moving towards the end of his life. I let out a deep sigh.

Christine and I had arranged a telephone appointment and I rang her at the agreed time. Once I had relayed all of Jack's impressions, I picked up her questions and began asking them.

'Jack, can you see anything at all?' I said.

In a moment I found myself looking out of his eyes. The view was dark and shadowy and he told me it was worse at night.

'Christine says she knows you do very well getting around, but she'd like to know whether you hurt yourself when you bump into things,' I said.

'Yes,' Jack answered. Then I felt bruises and frustration as he pictured hitting his head on the edge of a coffee table. I also saw an image of him struggling to get up the stairs.

'Do your eyes or your head ever hurt?' Christine wanted to know.

Once I'd asked Jack this question I felt my own eyes become sore and tingling. I could feel the urge to rub them, but this wasn't the main concern. As I looked at Jack's picture I could sense his head often hurt and that he was getting headaches from a high temperature. Then he pictured himself falling down and I felt the sensation of giddiness – he'd literally lost his balance.

'Is it painful when you cough?' asked Christine.

'Yes,' he said, giving me the feeling he had a chesty, hacking cough. As I pictured an energetic hologram of his lungs I could see there was something seriously wrong. It looked as though there was liquid in his lungs, or some sort of shadowing, and I could feel this was extending up into his throat.

'What is happening to your lungs?' I asked him.

'Drowning,' he replied.

I was beginning to be quite concerned and had to remind myself to be neutral again. It was important I didn't begin to analyse what the problem was or allow my brain to create a logical explanation. I needed to give Jack time to reveal information through his answers.

Christine's next question was: 'Do you have problems with your breathing?'

Again I felt his lungs as my lungs and that it was a struggle to take a full breath. With the possibility that Jack could have pneumonia, I told Christine it was essential she get in touch with her vet.

Christine told me she'd already taken Jack to the vet and she'd explain at the end.

'When you squealed in pain on Boxing Day, what was hurting you?' I said to Jack and in reply I felt pain in my right hip.

'Do you know what is wrong with you? Are you aware of your medical condition?' Christine had asked.

'Yes,' he said, 'I am aware.' Jack drew my attention to the areas of his body which were a concern. I sensed his kidneys were struggling. It also felt as if he had pneumonia or lung tumours and his head and throat were also a concern. I felt he could have tumours there as well. His hips were feeling very stiff from arthritis.

At this point Christine brought me up to date and explained what her vet had diagnosed. 'We took Jack to the vet's and they said he had a melanoma in his right eye – the one he told you was sore. I wanted to see what he would say about it, to see whether he could say whether it was malignant or not. I haven't told you this before, but my aromatherapist is intuitive like you and I asked her to ask Jack if we could remove his eye and he said the same to her as he did to you: he wasn't prepared for it to be done. We took him back about six months later and now the optical specialist has recommended his eye is completely removed, but given his age and the trauma it would cause, Paul and I have decided against it. Over the past few months he has really slowed down and started to cough for minutes at a time. So I took him to the vet's for an X-ray. It showed what we had feared – Jack has tumours in his lungs.'

It was such sad news, and while I was on the phone to Christine I could hear Jack coughing in the background. It was agonizing to listen to the deep, hacking coughs which went on and on. I asked Christine to leave the phone to go and comfort him; I couldn't bear him being on his own. I wondered whether Jack was aware of how sick he was. His final message in the previous communication had almost been like a goodbye speech, as if he was preparing Christine and Paul for his passing.

Once Jack had settled, Christine returned to the phone. 'His walks are limited to a few hundred yards through the country lanes now and a slow amble around the garden,' she said. 'He continually bumps into things. Anywhere outside his comfort zone of the house and garden is a struggle for him. Can you ask him if there is anything we can do to make life easier for him?'

'More cuddles and affection,' replied Jack, smiling for the first time. I also felt he'd benefit from pain relief, homoeopathy, healing and arthritis pain relief. So I suggested Christine try to contact a homoeopathic or holistic vet.

'I'm giving him healing,' said Christine, 'and my friend is too. Is there anything he wants to do?'

'Go to the sea, walk along the beach, feel the salty air one last time,' Jack said.

I repeated his words for Christine then the line went quiet and all I could hear was her softly crying.

'Is he aware of how we both feel about him, our concerns for his health and of course our love for him?' she said.

With a calm and steady voice, Jack replied. 'You are worried for me. You can see I am sad. My body hurts and I am trying my best to be jolly. Life is more difficult.'

'He *is* trying to be jolly. We can see that,' she said.

We'd now reached Christine's final question: 'How would you feel if we have to come to a decision about terminating your life?'

Jack was very clear. 'I am not ready yet. Not yet. I have longer still. Please help me, I don't want to go yet,' he said anxiously.

As I began to repeat what he had said for Christine I couldn't contain my feelings anymore. I loved this open-hearted gentle giant and I could feel Christine's pain knowing she might soon be losing him. As I repeated Jack's answer, sobs escaped between words and I was forced to focus on my breathing to calm myself down.

Christine didn't mind that I was upset; she knew I was fond of Jack. When I communicate with animals over a period of time I often find myself falling in love with them and then it's impossible to separate the working relationship from the loving relationship.

Paul had his own feelings about what was happening, which I'd learn much further down the line:

When Christine related this conversation it brought home to me just how effective the communication was. It was so real – I could visualize Jack saying just those words. It was also so close to our hearts – it gave answers to our questions, answers that we could understand and relate to, that were impossible to ignore. It was as if we were communicating with him directly. Agreed, Pea was the medium, but it felt like a one-to-one conversation (and I hadn't even spoken to Pea). It also became apparent to us that whatever we did thereafter had to be with Jack's consent and through mediation with Pea.

I returned home from work three days later and resumed my role of taking Jack for his daily walks. The following weeks were extremely difficult. The walks were by now very slow and very short. One day I took him for his morning walk to the country lane to do his toilet and halfway back he simply stopped and could go no further. I had to call Christine to bring our car to carry him home. I referred back to the feedback that Pea had provided in my absence and I could see that what she had described was perfectly reflected in Jack's demeanour and general condition.

Why did we go to an animal communicator and not back to the vet? We were in constant touch with the vet, she'd given us steroids for Jack and she left it to us to get in touch when we felt we needed to. Can you imagine spending years in the company of a deaf mute and then suddenly they can speak and hear? Imagine all the questions you'd have. We wanted to know how Jack was coping with his body's deterioration. Earlier communication with him had proved so enlightening that we felt that we needed to know as much about what was going on in Jack's head as in his body.

Ten days later Christine booked another communication with Jack and we fixed a telephone appointment.

'He's getting rapidly weaker and we both want to know how he's coping with his body's deterioration,' Christine said.

'OK. I can see from the questions you've sent me that you managed to take him to the beach,' I said.

'Yes, once Paul got back from the Middle East we took him together, just as Jack asked. He struggled a bit to get into the car, but you should have seen him when he reached the beach at Barry Island. He was amazing, he almost ran to the sand. He found a six-foot long log and carried it halfway round the beach. He looked so happy. Over the last few days he's been finding it hard to move, let alone walk up and down the lane. Yet even though the tide was out, and a long way from the promenade, he managed to make it to the water for a paddle.'

'That's fabulous,' I said gladly. 'All right, let's go through Jack's communication. The first thing he says is, "Not ready to go yet," but I can also sense he is feeling quite miserable. It does hurt to cough and his chest aches. His throat is also sore and this gets him down. When I asked him how he felt taking the steroids, he gave me the feeling of being a bit spacey.'

'Yes, he sometimes goes into a bit of a daze,' Christine interjected.

'Jack's requesting fish, and he's picturing white fish, and I feel this is because he feels sick in his stomach. He's giving me the taste of something metallic when he pictures food. I feel his taste buds have changed and food doesn't taste the same.'

'Can you ask him whether he enjoyed his trip to the beach?' said Christine.

'Yes,' said Jack, and he pictured a beach scene that was breezy and felt cold. 'A welcome escape,' he continued. 'I felt like I was in heaven.'

'I can see he can't stand easily now, but he keeps soldiering on,' I said.

'We gave him an ice cream and I could see how much happiness that one small thing gave him,' said Christine. 'Can you ask him whether he'd like to go back if the weather is good?'

'Yes, definitely,' Jack answered, 'but not when it's raining. Anything is better than this just waiting to die. I want an escape. Even if I lie down on the beach and die.'

I gave Christine some time to write down what Jack had said. She wanted to be able to give Paul the details of his communication.

'His coughing seems to have got worse, especially in the night, and we're interested to know whether it's more painful,' she said.

Jack gave me the feeling of his chest aching and that it was harder to breathe. I could feel these sensations in my own chest, which felt sore, and each breath was a struggle.

'I feel the only time he rests is when he is asleep. He gets headaches too. The way he describes the feeling in his chest is that he feels he is drowning,' I added.

'Does he want pain relief for his joints?' said Christine, remaining calm.

'He says his spine is sore and his hips and back legs ache, but he's more concerned with his chest, the headaches and feeling sick.'

I felt that my own head was about to crack open as I sensed that Jack was experiencing chronic headaches. 'Could you try putting a cold flannel over his head to give him some relief?'

'Yes, of course, we'll do anything for him,' Christine replied. 'The final question is really a message. Can you let him know we are worried for him and we can see he feels sad. We want him to know he doesn't need to be jolly for us, we understand.'

'He says he doesn't want to upset you and he also wants to have nice, happy moments with you at the end of his life. He is giving me the feeling that he will ascend soon and he's picturing where he'd like to be when he does.'

'The back room,' Jack said, showing an image of large windows. They looked like floor-to-ceiling doors. He pictured the sun and I knew he'd love to ascend in the sunshine. Then he pictured a needle and himself gently relaxing before there was another injection. He was making it clear what he hoped would happen.

I relayed it to Christine and she said, 'That's the kitchen. He loves lying in there because the sunshine pours in. He finds a spot on the floor where he's right in the middle of it. I've always felt that's where he'd want to be. As for the injection to relax his body before the second injection, we've already discussed it with the vet and that's what they've said they'll do.'

Jack was listening in to our conversation and urgently interjected, 'Not yet.'

There was one more thing Jack had said but I wasn't sure whether to share it until Christine shared her concern about the timing. Paul had been at home for the past month but he soon had to go away and there was nothing they could do about it.

Then I said, 'Jack's giving me an idea of when he may ascend, but animals can change their minds, so you need to see how Jack is feeling each day and play it by ear. I'm sure you'll feel it in your heart and know when it's time.'

'I'd like to know when he's saying, though,' she urged.

'He's actually giving two dates to me, 2 February and 10 February. He may mean either of these dates or he may mean some time between the two dates.'

'But Paul's going away on the ninth and he'll want to be there,' Christine replied.

'Well then, we'll just need to explain that to Jack and trust that he'll ascend when it's for his highest good, when it's the right time for him. You may find that Paul isn't present, but we'll have to leave that to Jack to decide,' I explained as gently as I could.

Early in the morning on 2 February my phone rang. It was Christine.

'I'm worried about Jack. He's having a bad day. He can't walk. He's just lying there. I remember he said the second might be the day he chose to leave. I don't know what to do, though, because even though he's struggling I don't quite feel it's his time,' she said with a calm strength. 'Could you ask him how he is feeling?'

'Yes, of course, I'll drop everything and do it this morning, then I'll call you back,' I said.

I connected with Jack through his photo.

'Hi, sweetheart,' I said, 'how are you?'

'I'm just tired. I wish Christine was with me all the time.'

'Are you in pain?' I said.

'Yes, a lot of pain,' he replied.

'Would you like that pain relieved?' I said.

'Yes. Why aren't they giving me pain relief? I don't want to go, I want to ease my pain,' he said.

I sensed sharp pains in his lungs and a heavy feeling in the solar plexus, the energy centre related to the sense of self, ego and power. I could also feel his hunger, yet however much he ate, this hunger wouldn't be satisfied.

'I want to be warm and comfortable,' he said. Then I saw an image of him finding it hard to get comfortable as he lay on the floor.

'Are you scared to go?' I said.

'Yes,' Jack replied.

'Do you see the light?'

'Yes, but I don't want to walk through the door.'

This seemed to be a metaphorical door and just a way for him to express that he wasn't ready to die.

'Are you staying on for your mother?' I referred to Christine.

'No.'

'Are you staying on for your father?' this time referring to Paul.

'No.'

'Do you feel like you're just existing?' For some reason I felt I needed to ask him this.

'Yes,' he said.

'Are you finding joy in life?' I said.

'No.'

'What's keeping you here, Jack?' I said, wondering why this dog who seemed to be suffering so much pain wouldn't allow himself to ascend to the light that was waiting for him.

'Fear,' he replied.

'What are you scared of?' I said.

'Not being here. I'm going to miss them,' and with those words I could feel his desperation. I broke down into tears as I sensed these tears were how Jack was feeling.

Once I'd regained my composure, I asked him, 'How can we help you over that fear?'

'Surround me in love.'

It was so simple.

'Just love me. Put your arms around me. Be close,' said Jack.

Christine said she understood what he was saying and she'd make sure he got everything he asked for. She would phone the vet for an appointment as soon as she was off the phone to me and she'd see about further pain relief.

A bit later I felt that I needed to check in with Jack again. When animals begin to die they can go so quickly. I wanted to be there for Jack so he could communicate his needs to his guardians. Christine was really happy about this and we agreed to talk later on.

When I rang her in the early evening, she said, 'You won't believe what he did. The minute I was on the phone explaining to the vet I'd like to take Jack over to discuss his pain relief but there was a problem because he couldn't walk, he got up and walked as though he'd been pulling a fast one on me.'

'What is he like?! That's great,' I said, laughing.

'He's been given some pain-relief tablets,' Christine explained.

Then I repeated Jack's communication for her: 'He feels more disconnected from his body, which he says feels great. He says he can think straight, he feels calmer and less worried or sad. He feels less panicky.'

I asked Jack when the right time was, wondering whether he'd made up his mind.

'Not yet. I want this night, this peaceful night. Tomorrow is another day,' he said, non-committally.

'He's taking each day at a time, living in the moment,' I told Christine. 'He says his body has relaxed and he's having his first proper sleep in ages.'

'He is. Yes. He seems so much more peaceful,' she said.

I let both Jack and Christine know I would be there for them and I told Christine not to hesitate to call at any time if she was at all worried. She was much calmer when we hung up the phone. She could see that Jack now had what he needed and he was much happier and relaxed than earlier in the day.

About 9.30 a.m. on 6 February she rang again.

'Jack's not doing so well. I think he's ready, Pea. Can you communicate with him? Ask him what he wants?'

'Yes, of course. I'll call you straight back,' I said, then I reached for Jack's photo. He connected with me straight away.

'I'm ready now,' he said. 'Everything is perfect, as it should be. Yesterday was too early. Tomorrow is too late. Feel secure in your heart; this is my perfect moment. All I ever wanted was to wait until now. Don't worry about the weather. I know it's not sunny, but you are my sunshine. You will always be my sunshine. I want to rest now. My body is tired. My resolve is weak. Everything is perfect and orderly.' Then he pictured a blue blanket. 'Just hold me,' he continued, 'I know everything will be all right. I'm not scared now. Angels have been talking to me. I know I'm going with them. They are all around me, waiting. It is very peaceful, very calm and very loving. I am ready now, Pea. Tell her I am ready.'

I rang Christine, who must have been waiting by the phone, and read Jack's communication to her, word by word, pushing myself to stay strong. Christine already knew in her heart; she was sensitive and intuitive, and she knew Jack well. She told me the previous night Sooty had gone into the dining room and spent the whole evening lying next to Jack, which was completely out of character for him. Jack had been spending much more time in there, but it wasn't a room Sooty would ever stay in. We talked about ways in which Christine and Paul could make Jack's ascension a beautiful celebration of his life with flowers, candles, music and his favourite things. We also talked about the relevance of the pale blue blanket, which turned out to be the pale blue throw Jack had had since he was a puppy. I reassured her Jack's ascension would be perfect because he was orchestrating it. All they had to do was honour his wishes. We hung up the phone and Christine started the preparations.

The loss of an animal I had been communicating with over a span of three years became all too much for me. I felt an agonizing sorrow, a similar pain to the one I had felt when I had received a call on Christmas Eve to inform me my granny had just died. It's the kind of grief that punches you in the gut and it's just uncontrollable. Many of my students ask me, 'How do you cope with the pain? I couldn't do what you do, I couldn't stand the pain.' Well, I'd be lying if I said it was easy. You feel the pain, you feel the agony and you feel the grief. With each animal I communicate with I give them a little piece of my heart. When they ascend, a piece of me goes to heaven with them. That's just how it is. But it's worth it, because every animal that can communicate their feelings helps them and their guardian. The pain is temporary and it's nothing compared to how the animal's guardian is feeling – their loss is always greater.

Days after Jack had ascended I heard from Christine:

Sooty sat in his usual spot, on top of the Aga cooker, and watched from a distance as Jack lay on his mat just inside the kitchen door in front of the glass windows. He was peaceful. He just laid his head between his paws and stared ahead. It took no more than a few minutes and he was gone. We wrapped him in his blue throw as he requested, which he always sat on over our snug sofa, then carried him to his grave in the garden. We lowered him as gently as we could into the deep hole. Just as we retrieved the ropes we'd used to lower him, his right paw fell out of the blanket. We added one of his teddies and Paul's rubber walking boots before covering his body with earth.

Looking back at the night before Jack ascended, it was as though Sooty had gone to him so they could say goodbye.

After Jack's ascension Paul did something that seems to be socially unacceptable for a man: he felt helplessly emotional and wept openly for weeks.

Then I received a card. Both Christine and Paul wanted to express thanks to those who had helped Jack, and them, through a difficult time. Inside, Paul had added a poem he'd written for Jack:

An Ode to Jack
Jumpin' Jack, Flash Feller,
Oh, the hearts you've won.
Your wagging tail,
Your giving soul,
Your coat like golden sun.
A gentleman of the canine world,
A friend to all you met,
You gave your love
Without condition
And no-one will forget.

This isn't the end of the story. Christine was able to share some magical moments she experienced *after* Jack's death:

Soon after Jack ascended, Paul had to return to work and I wasn't looking forward to being in the house without Paul and without Jack. My cousin suggested I stay with him in Christchurch, so I went the next day. He has a golden Labrador the same age as Jack, called Bagel. I was able to spend some wonderful therapeutic and quality time with Bagel, which felt like heaven.

One morning I was out for a long walk by myself when I came across a man throwing a ball for his dog. The dog was having so much fun, always catching the ball; he never missed it. I smiled to myself, as Jack had loved the same game and *never ever* missed a ball.

I continued walking for a while then found a lovely bench overlooking the water, where I spent some time just thinking about Jack. I was feeling quite melancholy. When I retraced my steps about 20 minutes later, the man was still throwing the ball for his dog. I was still thinking of Jack and feeling quite sad when the dog ran from one side of the field straight across to me on the other side. He stopped in front of me, looked me right in the eye and dropped the ball at my feet for me to throw it for him. He did this twice, and then carried on playing with his master. After I had thrown the ball the second time I looked at my watch and it was exactly one week – to the minute – since Jack had ascended. I had to sit down as I felt so emotional, and at that precise moment I received a text from my friend Sue, the aromatherapist, who had put simply: 'Thinking of you.'

When I saw this friend later I told her how timely her message had been. She told me that on that day she had been getting ready for her clients and had placed a heap of towels on the end of her treatment table. When she'd looked back at them, she'd thought she was seeing things – there were canine-sized paw indentations all across them. This was strange, because dogs aren't allowed in her treatment room, let alone up on the treatment table. She first thought that the towels just needed ironing, but when she took a closer look, sure enough, there were large paw prints, Labrador size, all down the length of the towels, and it made her think of me. So she sent me the text.

Later on, in the afternoon, my cousin's friend arrived with her black Labrador, Tommy, Bagel's brother. He spent at least an hour sitting beside me on the sofa, with his head on my lap or my leg. This apparently was out of character. My cousin's friend felt he must have known I needed some comfort, because it was so unusual. It wasn't a one-off either, as he sat with me three evenings in a row.

On my final evening before returning home, I was with four friends relaxing in the lounge after a late lunch. The two dogs, Bagel and Tommy, were fast asleep mingled amongst us on the sofas. Someone suggested we drink a toast to Jack. 'To Jack,' we all said, raising our glasses, and out of the blue Bagel's favourite toy squeaked very loudly from its position on the floor. Suddenly we all cried out, 'That must be Jack!'

Smiling and laughing, we held our glasses high, looking towards the toy, and said, 'Cheers, Jack!'

On 25 February, almost three weeks later, Christine asked if I could still communicate with Jack. I tried to begin the communication with the photo I had used when Jack was ill, but I immediately heard, 'Not that one, the other one.' The other photo was on the card Christine and Paul had sent me after Jack's ascension. It was a picture of a younger, healthier Jack, in a time before he had started to get sick.

'Thank you,' he said, referring to his ascension, 'it was graceful, it was peaceful, it was perfect … It was easy to let go, because I was ready. I love you so much for being brave and holding on. I know it wasn't easy for you. I just wanted as long as possible. Sooty and I shared a last moment together. He was always my cheerleader, despite how it looked. He tried to get me to meditate away from the pain as much as possible. When I went there were birds all around me singing. It was beautiful, warm and light. I felt so joyful again.'

Christine asked, 'While I was staying with my cousin in Christchurch and we toasted your life, was it you who made the toy squeak? Were you there?'

'Of course! I followed you. You know I like parties,' Jack said, and I saw a cheeky smile. 'Everything is perfect again,' he added, 'and I can run very fast and jump and bark. Everything is great. I'm always with you, in your heart, and we will see each other again when you come here. And we can play ball *all day*!'

CHAPTER 13

Spanish Explorer Joey

As I MADE further progress in animal communication, clients began to seek my services from countries around the world.

It was 16 January 2006 when Celia made contact from her home in Spain. Her cat, Joey, had disappeared. It was apparently quite normal for this Spanish explorer to go on his travels, but this time he'd been away for two days.

'OK, e-mail me his photo and I'll communicate with him straight away,' I replied.

Very soon there was another message and when I opened the attached document I found myself looking into the gentle face of a marmalade cat with an ivory chin and soft brushes of ivory through his burnt orange cheeks. Long white whiskers were framing his mouth and pale pistachio-green eyes looked across at something out of shot.

When I first began communicating with him I felt a sense of anxiety and sharp chest pains.

'Are you OK?' I said to him.

'No, I can't get out,' he replied.

'Where are you?' I said.

'I am in the basement. In the basement. By the boiler,' he replied. I could see an image of a small room with very little light; it was hard to see what was inside. What I could see was a concrete floor.

'Can you show me more of this place?' I said to him.

I immediately saw a door, then concrete steps. He pictured a dark green metal door hinged on the right with a handle on the left. He pictured himself in a dark empty space, lying by a wall. Above him at the top of the wall I could make out a horizontal window, which had horizontal bars. It was closed.

'Have you been in here all this time?' I said.

'Yes, since Monday,' he replied.

'How are you feeling?' I said.

My body went cold and I felt his feelings of frustration, thirst and hunger.

'Is this the basement where you live?'

'No,' he replied and I felt my heart ache. Then he showed an image of himself walking from inside one housing block to another. Even though there were two separate buildings above ground I sensed that their basements were joined underground. Joey explained he couldn't get back. He said he was very close to home and that his guardian lived 'next door'.

'Did you run away or was this an accident?' I said.

He chose not to answer the question directly, but he did say, 'Tell her I love her and I am very sorry. I am not a bad cat.'

Cats hardly ever admit if they've made a mistake – they have so much pride and dignity. As Joey hadn't been clear whether his situation was an accident or intentional, I then asked him the hardest question of all: 'Are you getting ready to ascend?'

'No, it's not my time,' he replied and I immediately felt my own relief.

'You are happy at home? You want to get back?'

'Yes, very happy at home,' he responded. 'Yes, I want to get back. I'm scared.'

'It's OK. I'll stay with you,' I reassured him. 'We'll keep our link open so you can always come through to me. You won't be alone anymore.'

I gave all the details from our communication to Celia over the phone: the basement, the green door, the adjoining basement, the housing block next door.

'The block next to me is uninhabited. You can't get in, it's all locked up,' she said, 'and the basement is probably empty.'

'Can you recognize his description of the window? It's at the top of the wall, it's oblong shaped and there are horizontal metal bars.'

'Yes. The windows to my basement are like that and so are the ones of the block next door,' she said.

'Could you reach him by going through from your basement?'

'No, there are only tiny gaps and it's quite a distance away,' she said.

'Then you'll have to get the block opened,' I said.

'I'll try, but it won't be easy,' she replied.

She spoke to the housing authority and after much delay and Spanish red tape, she was able to get hold of the person in charge of the block, but Mr Authority refused to open it. She rang him the next day and asked again and got the same answer. He wasn't going to budge.

'You've got to convince him,' I said to her. I was continuing to communicate with Joey and could feel him getting weaker and quieter. The days were passing by and he was frustrated. He didn't understand why it was taking so long.

'They just won't open it,' Celia said. 'What am I going to do?'

'Doesn't the man in charge like animals?' I said.

'No, he doesn't care and he's adamant he can't open it,' she replied.

'You'll have to make a plea to his heart,' I told her, 'because if you don't get in there soon Joey might not make it.'

Celia is a kind person who adores animals. She's the kind of human being you'd want to be with you through tough times because she'd stand by your side and support you. When it came to animals she was even more dedicated. She marched down to the local authority's office with her mother and put on the biggest show – partly acting but mostly real. She cried, she wailed, she begged, she pleaded and she ran the gamut from stroppy drama queen to helpless woman in need of rescue. She let the official see how worried she was and said that she would fall apart from the agony of not knowing if Joey was in there. Eventually, after a declaration of emotion any aspiring Oscar-winner would be proud of, Mr Authority crumbled and agreed to open the block.

In total it had taken four days to convince the local authority to give Celia access to the basement. Joey had now been without food and water for six long dark days.

There were two more frustrating hours waiting for the man with his key and then Celia walked inside and ran down to the basement. I had been able to tell her Joey was still alive, but he was weak and needed to drink as soon as possible. She was delighted to find he *was* there and he *was* alive:

> I picked up his weak, dehydrated ginger body and he melted into my arms. He was tired and hungry, but he looked up to my eyes as if to say, 'What took you so long?'
>
> When I was standing inside the basement I could see the back of the door was dark green, like you said, and the room was empty. There wasn't anything to drink and I'm not sure Joey would have lasted much longer.

Once Joey had had some time to recover from his ordeal, I communicated with him.

'Thank God Celia is such a stubborn woman,' he told me. 'I now love her more than I did before,' and I felt a huge feeling of love. 'Thank you for staying with me and encouraging the others. While you have a lot to learn, you are on the right path. Listen to your dog and cat more! Peace be with you. I want to rest now.'

Despite the fact I'd helped save his life, he still had the gumption to tell me off! That's cats for you! Still, he was right. I realized the more I learned, the more I didn't know. It felt as if I was standing at the tip of an iceberg with fathoms of information yet to be discovered.

Just before he dissolved our link, Joey offered me one last tidbit. 'We ginger cats are very spirited,' he said. Then he was gone.

CHAPTER 14

Sabre-Toothed Stewart

Two YEARS AGO, on a cold, pale blue day, I approached a Victorian house in London's 'Little India' on the south side of the river Thames, not knowing that this meeting would change my life forever. I was about to meet God in furry trousers.

I was visiting a home that consisted of humans, Belinda and Laura, and several cats. Belinda opened the door, dressed all in black with a drawn look on her face. After we had exchanged pleasantries, I walked over the threshold and my eyes locked onto a pair of eyes that in return locked onto mine.

'Wow!' I gasped. I suddenly felt short of breath. My legs were turning to jelly beneath me and I reached out to steady myself.

I was looking at the most intense eyes in a cat's body I had ever seen, and there was more. The cat seated in front of me, halfway up the stairs, had something incredible about him. I couldn't quite say what it was, but boy, I did know this – he was someone really special. And it wasn't because of his good looks,

206

even though he was a very handsome cat – chocolate and cappuccino tiger stripes, impressively long whiskers and the fluffiest feather-duster tail I had ever seen. Tufts of fur sprouted out between the pads of his oversized paws and a lion-like mane tapered to a neat point over his heart. His most striking features were the feather-like markings painted on his forehead, similar to those of Native American Mohawks, who wear three eagle feathers standing straight up on their 'Kahstowa' or feathered hat. I'd never seen a Maine Coon like him.

'Who are you?' I asked him. He looked like a cat, but I was certain there was more behind those ivory whiskers than met the eye.

He didn't reply, but Belinda told me he was called Stewart and was the fourth Maine Coon member of the house. The others were called Gypsy, Max and Beau. Stewart? It seemed an odd name for such a stunning cat.

'Right,' I said, catching my breath, my heart slowly returning to a steadier pace.

Belinda and Laura asked me to communicate with Stewart to see how he was feeling and just for a general check-up, not because of any underlying concerns of a behavioural or physical nature. They settled in the sitting room on a green two-seater sofa and Stewart lounged over the back cushion behind Laura's head. I positioned myself on the other sofa opposite them. Stewart began by introducing himself and then he launched into what he wanted to say, ignoring the questions they'd already prepared. I should have known from the moment I laid eyes on him that he would call the shots.

He sent me feelings of emotion and I sensed dignity and tolerance. He then sent me energy thought-forms as he explained the foundation of this emotion.

'I see them struggling, failing, behaving inappropriately, and understand that this is because they are less evolved spiritual beings.'

'He has quite a high opinion of himself then!' said Belinda.

I thought to myself, *I've never met a cat who's said that before.* And he didn't stop there.

I asked him, 'What's your job here in this house, Stewart?' I thought this would be revealing, believing he must have a job that was more interesting than 'chief mouse-catcher'. But I wasn't prepared for his answer:

'To introduce you to higher vibrations.

'To connect you to yourselves.

'To connect you to energy.

'To connect you to love.

'To connect you to your heart.

'To challenge your understanding of life.

'To oversee your spiritual journey.'

My God, I thought.

Laura seemed frozen to the spot and for a moment was speechless. Then she asked me to repeat what he'd said, maybe wanting to check that she'd heard correctly.

I tried to ask another question, but at this point Stewart said directly, 'It's not about questions. This is about their journey. I have been waiting for this time.'

I knew better than to push him for something he didn't want to express and gave him the stage. 'What would you like to say?'

Without a moment's pause Stewart got straight to the point. 'Look at yourselves. You are letting your life slip by. Where is your heart? What is important to you? Why are you not living life through your heart? I know you are not happy. I feel your sadness, your indecision and your confusion. Ask not, "What should I be doing?" Ask, "What will make me happy?" And follow this direction with all your heart, and your soul will fly free and soar. I know you are walking around in the mud. Look down at your feet, they can hardly move.'

Stewart sent me a picture of two feet trying to wade through thick heavy mud. Belinda let out an audible sigh and lowered her gaze to the floor.

'Raise your eyes now. Listen to the birds, the trees, the sun, the Earth – these are qualities you need. These qualities will raise your vibration and life will seem easy once more.'

While he sent me these thought-forms, he also sent me a picture of trees caught in the sunlight. I heard the sounds of birds singing and felt soft warm grass under my feet.

I looked at his guardians. They were still with me, but quiet. Belinda came across as a hard-working driven woman who looked tired, while Laura seemed more bubbly and smiley. At this point, I didn't know how they were taking the communication. Even though I'd proven my connection with Stewart by going through some details, I was unsure if they were able to accept what he was saying now.

Finally Belinda spoke. 'It makes sense. I'm going through a difficult time with work at the moment. So I guess life is like that.'

Stewart continued, 'Remember back to your childhood. What did you desire? What made you happy? Why did this change?'

We all sat in silence again for a while as they contemplated Stewart's message. I don't think any of us were prepared for his communication. Laura questioned why he didn't like to spend any time with them and why he didn't enjoy fuss like their other three cats. She wanted to know why he appeared angry with them.

My own thought was, *Because he's not like the other cats*, but Stewart wanted to answer these questions himself.

'You ask if I am angry with you. Yes, I am angry with you. In a frustrated way.' I felt a huge wave of frustration within my own body. 'Why do humans block the truth? Sit down and listen to my heart.' Stewart sent me a picture where he guided Belinda and Laura's hands to touch his body either side of his heart. And with this image in their minds, he said, 'I honour you. For all that you are and all that you can be. Our souls go way back. We were family in another life. I am *glorious*. Bask in my beautiful energy. Let it soak into your pores. Open your hearts and reach out to me with love.'

In my mind, Stewart's voice sounded no-nonsense but very poised. He exuded an overwhelming serenity and a confident charm that said, 'I know who I am.' He didn't need affection and didn't feel the need to constantly give it. His love was in his heart and that was enough.

Connecting with him was easy because he had a very strong energy. However, I soon learned he'd only share what he wanted you to know. He wasn't an open book, where you could flit from this page to that and put it down when you got bored of it. Stewart demanded your respect.

'He tells me there are three things he wants you to change,' I told Belinda and Laura. Stewart was speaking more slowly now, giving me time to receive his thought-forms and write his words down accurately before I repeated them out loud:

'1. *Your breath:* Breathe more deeply to connect with energy.

'2. *Your outlook:* Only think positive thoughts.

'3. *Your agenda:* Follow your heart on all matters.'

Belinda and Laura scrabbled about for some paper and asked me to repeat what he'd said.

'He's got a point,' Laura said, taking in the enormity of his suggestions. 'How does he feel physically? Is he OK?'

'His back feels sore. From the middle, working backwards. It feels bruised, like he's had a fall. His spine is quite sore around there.'

When I reached this part of his body I had seen flashes of red and my own lower back had ached. I wanted to share what I'd received from Stewart as sensitively as possible. He had also drawn my attention to his heart; it seemed enlarged and the heart wall looked thicker than I sensed it should be. I knew I wasn't able to tell for certain whether this was the case, and rather than rely solely on my impressions, I would advise them to consult their vet for a professional diagnosis.

When I gently suggested Stewart was drawing my attention to his heart, Belinda immediately responded, 'Oh yes. He has an enlarged heart. We know about it. He's on pills for his blood pressure. He's got HCM, hypertrophic cardiomyopathy.'

This meeting with Stewart, and more importantly his communication, absolutely blew me away. It wasn't the usual conversation I'd have with a cat, in fact any animal. I thanked Stewart for his time and patience and said my goodbyes, leaving his guardians to soak in his messages.

A month or so later, I was climbing out of my car and, with freezing winter hands, ringing the doorbell at Belinda and Laura's house again. Today they'd asked me to communicate with a different member of the pride, Max, a striking charcoal-black and snow-white tuxedo cat with paws dipped in marshmallow. I'd asked him to be at home, telling him what time I'd turn up, and sure enough, there he was, draped over the top cushion of the window armchair. He shared the news that he had a girlfriend and, through a little detective work, going on his directions and description, Belinda and Laura worked out who his feline beloved was. After they'd asked all their prepared questions, they turned and asked Max if there was anything else he wanted to share. It turned out to be the most important question of all.

'Tell them not to worry about me. Stewart's the main concern – keep an eye on him. The rest of us are all right really,' he said.

We all looked at one another, wondering what was wrong. This communication became a pivotal moment that would change the lives of Stewart and his pride forever.

I was invited upstairs to see Stewart, whom we found lying flat out on the spare bed. He rubbed his head against my hand and then angled it back so I could rub his chin. Belinda commented how unusual this was. When he looked into my eyes, I tried to body scan him, but I felt a block. Now I look back at this moment, I am sure he didn't want me to find out what was wrong and was preventing it. I found his loud motor purr and ardent desire for affection distracting and wasn't able to sense a problem beyond a sore lower back.

After my visit, Belinda and Laura insisted on running their hands through Stewart's fur, despite his protestations, and discovered a lump the size of a pea on his left flank. Concerned about what Max had said and this new discovery, they took him to be checked out and a biopsy was scheduled. The result wasn't good: Stewart had cancer.

When Belinda e-mailed me the news, I felt as though I was falling through a dark hole with a pressing heaviness over my chest. I was almost winded by the diagnosis. It didn't matter that Stewart wasn't my cat, we had a special connection and I had fallen in love with him. *Not Stewart, please not Stewart,* I thought. I wasn't the only one to feel a special bond with him – everyone who had met him had an identical response. He had people from all walks of life mesmerized. It wasn't only what he said or the guidance he gave that made him different from other cats. It was as if he was teaching through *being*, and he was able to touch people in a very deep way.

Shortly after the biopsy, the vet opened him up and found the cancer had spread further than she'd imagined. She cut out the cancerous tissue and some of the surrounding area in an attempt to prevent the cancer cells from returning.

I visited Stewart shortly after he'd returned home. His strong energy had vanished and he looked exhausted and weak as he crouched, tight and hunched, on a blanket on the living-room floor.

Belinda and Laura knew I was a Reiki practitioner and asked me to channel healing to him. After about 30 minutes I saw him begin to relax, his body letting go of tension and pain, until he rolled upside down with his chin exposed and a sparkle in his eyes. This was more like him. During this time we shared a silent but profound connection. It's impossible to describe it other than to say it was like oneness – togetherness on a very deep and heartfelt level.

It was April 2008 and the prognosis was grim. He'd been given two, possibly three months. Thankfully, he had other ideas. After a few healing sessions and check-ups at the vet's, he began to regain his strength and communicate his feelings. He asked us all to remain very positive and loving, not only to him but also to the other cats, one another and ourselves. He seemed to be communicating from a higher consciousness – it was as if he knew the bigger picture and wasn't worried about the present. He didn't want anyone to feel sorry for him and said he intended to be around until after Christmas. Belinda and Laura were delighted.

They asked me to channel Reiki to him on a regular basis. Sometimes he would welcome it and sometimes not. 'I don't need it,' he'd tell me with smiling brown lips and he'd saunter off into another room or, if he was lying outside soaking in the sunshine, he'd simply move chair. He was always kind in his clarity, and healing was never forced upon him. Stewart always called the shots, because he knew his body better than anyone. If he didn't want it, he didn't want it, and that was good enough for me. Although on one occasion I foolishly challenged his judgement.

'Come on, Stewart, how about some Reiki?'

'No,' he said, giving me a disapproving Paddington Bear-like stare.

I was quick to learn and didn't make that mistake again.

It was during this time with Stewart that I realized I should take my Reiki practice all the way and be attuned to Master level. A few months later I completed my Master-level training.

Stewart remained incredibly strong, both in mind and body. After considering the options, Belinda and Laura decided not to put him through chemotherapy. They felt it was a lot for him to go through and they had been advised it might only buy him a few extra weeks. Once they'd decided on this, Stewart himself communicated that he really didn't want it. He said he knew he wasn't going to live forever and he wanted his remaining time with the family to be as peaceful as possible.

Life went on. Despite the growing lump on his side, Stewart carried on as normal, jumping onto the kitchen worktops looking for fish, leaping over wooden fences and going out on neighbourhood patrol. When one of the other members of the pride annoyed him, he'd give them a quick swipe to remind them of their place. He was adamant no one was to be miserable or negative about his illness. He asked for Belinda and Laura to think positively and to see him as healthy and well. He said this would help him and told me I was to do the same. I never felt he preached, but he did teach all of us through these conversations. He was helping us to view disease and the end of life issue in a different light.

I began to notice other changes. Belinda had completely taken to heart Stewart's earlier messages and had been working on her thought patterns and outlook on life. She became more cheerful and less stressed, until one day she walked in the front door and I nearly didn't recognize her. There stood a woman with an illuminated face, full of happiness and vibrant, light energy. Where had Belinda gone and who was this woman impersonating her? The change was startling and she said it was all down to Stewart.

'How can I carry on being miserable when he is fighting cancer and being so positive? He's an inspiration,' she said.

Belinda also began to wear colours that reflected her lighter side, alongside her wardrobe of doom and gloom black. Laura was also more positive and became more interactive in Stewart's communications. The energy in the house also changed and whenever I was visiting I found it peaceful and calm, almost still. The fast, fractious, worrisome energy of earlier months had dissolved away. Instead of being destroyed by the news that the leader of the pride was terminally sick, the house became one of abundant love, sharing, giving and kindness. It could have been the happiest place in London. All of this originated from Stewart, who refused to be down or miserable. He would beam a beacon of love into the heart of everyone he came across. He was very strong and very knowing. It was as though he was drawing on knowledge thousands of years old – almost as if he were the Dalai Lama of the cat world. He was a true inspiration.

His vets continued to be astounded by his progress. The tumour was getting bigger, but he appeared so well and cheerful. He would jump up onto the high surgery table by himself and was always very amenable, despite the pokes and prodding. The vets fell in love with his gentle nature and easy-going ways.

The tumour was now very visible, like a satsuma on his left flank, and had begun to spread down both his left and right leg and up along his spine towards his head. Yet it didn't appear to bother him in the slightest. Stewart was such a determined cat. In a different lifetime, I imagined him as a sabre-toothed tiger, fearless and powerful. Whenever Belinda and Laura asked for a communication with him, he was extremely positive and reminded them to be the same. Sometimes he was cheeky, but mostly he was considerate and kind, guiding them gently along the journey from his diagnosis to the anticipation of his too-early death. He was a very courageous animal.

As people were scuttling about buying Christmas trees and fairy lights, I was sitting in Belinda and Laura's living-room and Stewart was sleeping upstairs. It was now seven months after his initial diagnosis. Today I was communicating with Max. He was lying across the top of the window armchair, his favourite position. He was feeling very sad about Stewart, whom he saw as a father figure, even though Max was four years old and Stewart only seven. I felt a heaviness in Max's heart. He wanted to reassure Belinda and Laura that he would take on the role as leader of the family, but he didn't want Stewart to leave.

'What can we do to help Stewart?' both Laura and Belinda wanted to ask. Max appeared to be the feline healer of the family and was always around Stewart, either licking him or just being nearby. He was the only cat Stewart would let really close. And of course he had drawn our attention to Stewart being unwell in the first place.

'Give him comfort. Clear the energies. Remove all negative thought. Be careful what energy you bring into the house. See him as well. See him as getting better and focus on it. Love him as his complete and perfect self, every day. Do not feel sorry for him. Admire his strength and determination. Bring him comfort in his dying need. He will let you know.'

Stewart purred through Christmas. The whole family went to their residence on the Isle of Wight, the island of his birth and the place he called home. He saw London as the place he lived when he wasn't where he preferred to be. He enjoyed all the visitors, celebrations and present opening. This was what he had wanted to see, to be part of, with his pride all around him.

After Christmas they returned to London and I was called again. As I sat on the sofa in the living room, Stewart lay on top of the cushion behind my head, on an oversized soft fleece Santa hat, preferring the large red point to the white fur trim. Occasionally he stood up and kneaded it with his paws while at the same time purring in my ear. He was relaxed and smiling, as I sat with Beau, the big ginger cat, draped across my lap.

It was Beau's turn for a communication with Belinda and Laura, but while I sat relaying his answers to their questions, I could feel Stewart's presence, his energy, as a strong force behind me. At one moment I had to stop speaking because I was having what I could only describe as a spiritual experience. It wasn't really something I could put into words, more a feeling. This moment with Stewart behind me, purposely close to my right cheek, felt divine. If was as if a huge gentle energy radiated from Stewart and took me out of my physical human existence and let me experience a lightness and bliss I'd never felt before. It was always his *presence* that had the most profound effect on me, not what he did or even what he said. It was his *being*. It was as though a bright beacon of light was shining out of every pore, soaking those he loved from head to foot in divine bliss.

At the end of the communication I remained seated, pinned to the sofa by a round ball of ginger fluff purring away. Stewart was still lying across the top of the cushion. He reached forward and rested his large Maine Coon paws on my shoulder. It felt exquisite. This was the first time he had deliberately reached out to touch me and it would be the last. It was a powerful moment; his touch was full of love and reassurance.

Laura said in jest, 'Could you get any closer to Pea, Stewart?'

He had my full attention now, and with his mouth practically next to my ear, he whispered. 'Tell them they will know I am ready to leave when my aura is too big for my body.'

We didn't know what this meant, but we trusted it would become clear at the right time. Belinda and Laura's concern had been the same as that of many guardians: 'How will we know when he's ready to leave?' I told them not to worry, both Stewart and Max were reassuring them they'd know when it was time and Stewart had already been clear that he'd need assistance to ascend. That was one less thing to worry about.

On 2 February, London was covered in a deep pristine white blanket of sparkling snow and everywhere came to a standstill. Dogs ran barking with joy and I sculptured a snow-kitty on my back lawn.

Not long after this Belinda and Laura came home to discover Stewart had licked his side and there was an open wound. They called me to visit him. When I walked in, he was lying on a chair by the kitchen sink, with floor-to-ceiling glass doors behind him and a view out to the tiny backyard with the cat-climbing frame. He was wearing the plastic buster collar he had worn over 10 months earlier. He looked a sorry sight, with his long white whiskers drooping down either side of his chin and the saddest look in his eyes. This was the most forlorn I'd seen him since the operation.

I bent down in front of his chair and two intense straw-coloured eyes stared back at me. At that moment I knew he couldn't fight the cancer anymore. I could tell that in her heart Laura knew too. She was spending more time with him than Belinda was and I think she had sensed how he had changed.

'Why are you licking yourself sore?' I asked him.

'I want to remove it,' he said, a heavy sadness in his voice. My heart ached hearing him like this.

When I looked at his side the mass appeared to be breaking out from his skin, weeping and pink. Occasionally he tried to reach and lick it, but the collar stopped him and, defeated, he lowered his head. His resignation was almost palatable. This heavy sadness was such a stark contrast to his earlier positivity.

Stewart willingly accepted healing and after 50 minutes I thought I'd channel healing to his head and moved my chair to the front of him, but it was the wrong decision, because Stewart struggled up and slowly edged his legs round until his back was facing me again. By the time the healing ended he was looking peaceful lying across the chair and when Laura came back in he asked for some food.

But the wound didn't heal and twice Stewart was taken to the vet's to have fluid drained from the tumour. Each time he returned home he was brighter and more relaxed, but just over a week later Belinda contacted me to say he seemed really down again and they didn't know what to do.

I knew they were wondering whether it was time to put him to sleep. They needed to hear from Stewart himself. 'Let him share the responsibility and express what it is he's feeling and thinking,' I advised them. We agreed that over the weekend they would send me some questions for Stewart and I would communicate with him on the Monday. However, Stewart didn't want to wait. That evening, while I was in the kitchen making my supper, he suddenly broke into my thoughts and told me he was very nearly ready to go, he just wanted one more thing – 'a trip back home' to the island. Feeling how close he was to ascending, I was overwhelmed with sadness.

On Monday we communicated again.

'My heart is ready. It's tired,' he said. 'But I want another two weeks – wait for the sunshine, please.'

Even though we were discussing the end of his life, Stewart wasn't miserable. His energy came across as peaceful, almost ethereal. He sounded steady and in control.

'I only really wanted to get past Christmas,' he said. 'This has been extra time. Don't worry, it's not as bad as it looks. You humans are so emotional and negative. I often meditate away from the pain. It is a great joy to do this and very comforting.'

I felt in awe of his approach to his own death. It wasn't so much what he said, it was more what he didn't say. I can't remember one time when he complained about his lot. There was never a 'Why me?', 'It's not fair', 'I don't want to die' or 'I'm scared.' Stewart was always upbeat and in the moment. Once again he reminded Belinda and Laura to be happy. He wanted to enjoy each day with his pride, as he saw them, until those days came to an end.

Within a few days, Belinda, Laura and the rest of the pride were on a ferry to the Isle of Wight – Stewart's island. They e-mailed to let me know he had relaxed the moment he got there. I thought this would be a good time to check in with him.

'How do you feel about being on the island?'

'*Free!*' he shouted and I felt the wonderful sensation of his joy. This was only the second time he'd shouted anything. The first was when he had said, 'I am *glorious.*' I could feel he was happy and enjoying life.

Then I asked him the practical question that Belinda and Laura had wanted to broach: 'Are you happy being buried at the breeder's?' This was an impolite way of describing the home of a lady who adored Maine Coon cats and bred them. Stewart was one of her original kittens and she loved him.

'Yes, this is what I want,' he replied. 'Let my body disintegrate into the ground, as it did before. This is natural, as it needs to be. I am mirroring my previous life. There is no need to hang on to any part of me, let me go back to earth. Let my sky energy and Earth energy be reunited.'

Stewart spent three sunny days on the island, jumping over fences to reach neighbours' gardens then leaping up to the roof of a shed, where he sat lookout with the other three cats positioned in a circle around him, as if keeping guard and offering protection to their great leader.

On Monday 2 March, exactly one month since the snowfall, the family returned to London with Stewart crying in the car, something he'd never done before. He also began to struggle to breathe, making a strange rasping noise. Within a matter of days, the cancer had advanced so much he was carrying a tumour the size of a crab apple on his side, and the vet suggested it was time to let him go.

Belinda had to go to work, but within a few minutes she was on the phone asking whether I could communicate with Stewart to see what he wanted. I dropped everything, found his photo and looked into his magnificent all-knowing eyes. I wrote down everything he said and rang Belinda back.

'I felt his lungs are filling with fluid,' I told her.

'Yes, that's what the vet thought too,' she replied.

'He wants to go now,' I said, then fought back tears as the reality of this hit me. I don't think anyone can ever be fully prepared for this moment, despite seeing it advancing.

'That's all we needed to know,' said Belinda, in an almost monotone voice. I knew her well enough to know she was trying to remain strong as she sat with work colleagues nearby.

'Would you like to hear the rest of what he said?'

'Yes, if that's OK.'

But as soon as I tried to get the words out, I began to sob. Hot tears poured down my cheeks. A silence went down the line as I found it impossible to speak without crying. I felt so unprofessional and tried to fight off the pain. I reminded myself this was their cat, not mine, and I was meant to support them, especially now, as they prepared to say goodbye to one of their best friends.

I thought I sensed Belinda crying too, but she was also trying to hold it together. 'I don't want him to suffer,' she said. 'All we wanted to know was whether he was ready.'

While she was talking I got myself back together and was able to carry on. 'He is ready to go tonight,' I said. 'He pictured an open door with light pouring down. He feels the light

224

pulling him. He is only hanging on "to make sure". He says, "I need to know in their hearts they are ready. I am not crying – do not cry for me because you think I am crying. I miss my island, I want to go back there."'

His energy felt weak, as if he was already letting go and beginning to drift away. I could see gold rays all around him, shining outwards from his body.

'Put the fire on, get the daffodils out, play some of that nice music,' he instructed. 'Say quiet, peaceful prayers. Positive thoughts.'

I channelled Reiki to Stewart from 6.10 p.m. to 6.40 p.m. that night, but I felt a change at 6.29 p.m. The energy in between my hands, as I held his photo, changed from a strong pull to a drifting, lighter sensation – Stewart had ascended.

At 7 p.m. I received a text from Belinda: 'He has gone, in body at least.'

The following day Stewart's final wish was honoured. Belinda and Laura took a ferry to the Isle of Wight, to the garden of his birthplace, and laid his tired body to rest in the earth. His life had gone full circle and now he was able to return to his original form. The sabre-toothed tiger in him was free.

CHAPTER 15

'The Doggie Guide to Stardom'

by Marmite

THE SUN WAS streaming in through the window, causing a reflection on my computer screen. I had just returned from four days away and was reading through a long list of e-mails when one name jumped out at me – Nikki – and then when I checked my answer phone for messages I heard a voice jump out at me – Nikki's:

I'm sorry I have to contact you, but very sadly Marmite has gone missing again. I know that almost exactly one year ago you were able to help us find him and I'm hoping that you may be able to do the same again.

'Marmite,' I whispered to myself. I remembered his nine-year-old Jack Russell face, his coffee-coloured eyes and sense of fun. He lived with his guardian, Nikki, and her partner on a farm in Staffordshire, not far from a quarry. I dialled her and asked, 'Is he still missing?'

'Yes,' she answered anxiously. 'We've been looking for him down rabbit holes every day. We've nearly dug up half the quarry! I've even hired a thermal imaging camera and been probing holes with it in case I could pick up Marmite's heat. It's been seven days now.'

'Seven days!' I repeated with concern. I thought back to the year before, when Marmite had gone off on an adventure. He'd been missing for seven days then, too, and we'd been lucky to find him alive. 'What happened?' I prompted.

'I was away on holiday with my mum and Marmite was staying with my dad in their house, which is right next door to my barn conversion. He likes to stay there on and off, so it's a familiar arrangement. At 4 a.m. he woke Dad up to let him outside. When Dad called him he didn't come back, so he left the patio door open, expecting him to return. When he got up in the morning he saw he wasn't there. He hadn't come home.'

'OK,' I said calmly, 'I'll communicate with him straight away, then I'll phone you back.'

We hung up. I knew by gut instinct that I needed to communicate with Marmite quickly. Through experience I've learned it is better to approach every missing animal case by using a photo to link in with them, rather than visiting the location. In any case, Nikki and Marmite were based over 100 miles away from my home in London.

Nikki e-mailed me Marmite's photo and I printed it out. Holding it, I could see the wildly sprouting tan and white hair surrounding his eyes. Immediately he was transmitting loud and clear, as if my radio had just been tuned to the right frequency. The rest of my world faded away and there was just one focus, like a bright beam of light illuminating the way. Details came like artillery fire, one moment through a word I'd hear in my head, then through an emotion I'd feel, then through an image I'd see in my mind, like those pictures we see when we're dreaming. I tried to capture every impression as it came at bullet-speed:

- Confident. Bold. Fearless.
- Big adventurer.
- Will follow sniffs, travelling long distances.
- Had been sleeping curled up on the sofa and end of the bed.
- Woke Nikki's dad up by walking over him.
- Went to back door, hinged on right. Dad let him out.
- Went about sniffing, then peeing.
- Then decided to go through wooden fencing and across field.
- Street safe – knows to avoid cars
- House and barn conversion overlook fields.
- Fascinated by holes and wants to explore them.
- Will chase a rabbit into a hole until he gets stuck.

After these impressions Marmite began to share the impor-tant details, the facts that could help us locate him.

'Where are you now?' I said to him, as I held his photo and looked into his eyes.

The first image I saw in my mind was of Marmite standing on his back feet pawing at something above him. I could make out it was something solid and grey. He appeared to be struggling to get out of this place, and I felt in my own body the exhaustion he was feeling in his. Despite his determined efforts, the way out was far above him and he couldn't reach it.

With experience I've realized that with such cases there's an element of sensing the guardian's fear, which is a strong emotion. So to be sure that what I feel is from the animal and not the guardian it's essential I double-check by moving my awareness inside the animal's body. So I imagined a tiny version of myself slipping inside the top of Marmite's head and down into one of his paws. Immediately I could feel he was cold and hungry – my own hands felt cold and my stomach ached. Looking out of his eyes and down at his paws, I could see water. He was standing in water.

'Where are you stuck?' I said.

Marmite gave me a picture of a wooded area and a slope.

'Are you stuck down a drain?' I said to him.

In response I saw a picture of what looked like cement surrounding him. It seemed drain-like and really tight.

'Show me the opening,' I said.

Immediately I was looking up through his eyes, from the darkness, to a small area above emitting a glimmer of daylight. Marmite was far down beneath the surface of the earth.

I needed to see what the exit of this prison was like, so set my intention to leave Marmite's body and hover above the place where he was trapped.

Hovering in the air outside the entrance, I saw weeds and overgrowth, nothing distinctive at all. This was a depressing realization. How was I going to advise Nikki where to look? I mentally zoomed out a little to see more of the surrounding area and everywhere looked much the same – brambles and overgrowth. In fact, I couldn't even see the opening to where Marmite was trapped.

'What is the opening like?' I said. 'How do we get you out?'

That was when I saw a metal grille about two feet wide.

I returned to Marmite, slipping my awareness inside his head again and noting what I felt. He was cold and shivering, but he was relieved. He knew he wasn't alone anymore.

Looking out of Marmite's eyes once more, I could tell he was really deep down, not just a few feet. No sunlight was reaching where he stood. I was worried by the thought of him being trapped in this grim, prison-like cell, but I knew from experience I needed to remain calm and neutral, otherwise I'd be no help to him at all.

'How far are you from home?' I said.

'A mile,' came his reply.

'Which direction did you head in when you left Nikki's parents' home?'

'To the left,' he said and I saw an image of him racing through wooden fencing and dashing across a field towards a group of trees.

Then he gave me some information to reassure Nikki. 'Tell them to come across the field to the left,' he instructed, 'and not to give up searching. I'll be home soon. Tell them to open the door.'

I felt Marmite was a tough guy, a fighter, not the type to give up easily. I also felt he was urging me to contact Nikki to relay what he'd communicated.

Nikki answered the phone and I began going through Marmite's communication. When I told her there was water running over his paws, she said, 'There's no water around here. No streams or rivers or anything. It's just a sand quarry.'

'There's definitely water where he is,' I said. 'This place is deep down, about eight feet or more. There's no direct daylight but a feeling of daylight high above. It feels as though he's surrounded by cement or something like that. It's not a rabbit hole and it's not in sand – this is man-made. The opening is about one to two foot wide, but it's covered in brambles and weeds, so it won't be easy to see it. You'll need to pull the weeds back.'

'I can't think *where* that is,' Nikki said in a distracted way.

'He's shown me that he went through the wooden fencing outside your house and across the field, then up to the left. He's about a mile away. Can you think of a water source about a mile away?' I asked her.

There was a long silence on the line. Then she exclaimed, 'I think I know where it is! There's an old lock not far away. I've called for him there already, but I didn't search the area. I didn't even know that there was a shaft down there. The trouble is, he won't bark, even when he's stuck. How will I know exactly where he is?'

'As soon as we're off the phone I'll communicate with him and let him know how important it is that he barks,' I said.

231

'I need to call my partner so he can come home and look after our baby and then I'll go straight out,' Nikki said. Then the phone line went dead. She was already acting on the information.

I linked in with Marmite again and told him Nikki was on her way. I felt his sense of relief and joy. Then I explained that he needed to bark because the entrance to his location was hard to find. I said to him, 'This is *really* important. We may only have this one go at finding you, so if Nikki is close, if you hear her, you have to bark as loudly as you can.' Marmite agreed. I told him how much Nikki loved him and how much I loved him and repeated that people were on their way to find him. Then we ended the communication and I carried on with life at home, not expecting to hear anything until the next day.

One hour later the phone rang. As I picked up the receiver, I heard Nikki screaming.

'You've done it again! You've found him! We've got him! He's here, Pea!'

'You've found him?' I could hardly believe it myself. 'So quickly?'

'Yes, he was there. Where you said he'd be. As soon as I approached the entrance I heard him barking and he hasn't stopped since. Can you hear him?' she said, moving her mobile towards his direction.

There was the sound of excited yaps.

'Can you hear him?' she said again.

'Yes, I hear him.'

'He's barking and I'm shouting down to him, telling him he'll be OK,' she explained.

'He's not out yet?' I became concerned.

'No, we can't reach him. It's got to be about 10 feet deep,' said Nikki.

'It's really important you get him out tonight,' I said firmly.

'Yes, we will. I don't know how, but we won't leave him. I just can't believe we found him so quickly. Why didn't I call you a week ago?' she said, shouting with joy.

'Call the fire brigade if you have to. He's weak and hungry, Nikki, he needs to get out today.' I wanted to break through her euphoria to make sure the message hit home. I couldn't bear the thought of Marmite stuck all by himself for an eighth night at the bottom of a cold, hard, pitch-black cement cell.

'I will, I will. I won't leave without him. Thank you so much. Bye.'

And she was gone.

I realized my legs were trembling and I had to sit down. The thrill of finding an animal who would otherwise surely have died can't be put into words. It is something to be felt with the heart and the body. I was amazed it had happened so fast. That dynamo dog, Marmite, had communicated so clearly with me, even while scared, hungry and all on his own. He'd managed to give me the most important details so we were able to find him.

The next morning Nikki gave me a full report. Despite her own efforts and those of her partner and mother, they'd been unable to get Marmite out of the ground, so had called the fire brigade. A fire engine full of strapping uniformed hunks had helped rescue her small Jack Russell and one fireman had told her it was the most unusual case they'd ever received; they'd never heard of a 'pet psychic' locating a dog before.

Marmite had been trapped at the bottom of a 12-foot shaft below the sluice gate of a disused canal. About a foot from the entrance the cement-like blocks slanted to a vertical drop, making it impossible for him to get out, even if he had been tall enough to reach, and also impossible for anyone to be lowered down to him. Instead the fire brigade lowered a plastic bucket into the hole, which was only a foot in diameter, hoping he would jump into it, but he was unsure and refused to get inside, despite cajoling from above. As the shaft was so narrow, a plastic bucket was all that would fit and it was a case of persevering. The firemen tried again, but still Marmite ignored the bucket. Then Nikki had the idea of putting his bed into it. The firemen lowered it down and this time Marmite jumped straight in!

A thinner and dishevelled version of Marmite was hauled up and out of the shaft and into Nikki's waiting arms. He was blinking and disorientated, but overjoyed to see her, licking her face and squirming with excitement and relief. She took him home to feed him and give him all the comforts he'd need after his week-long ordeal in the underground prison. Everyone was overjoyed and treated him to a hero's welcome – except, that is, for Crumpet, his two-year-old Jack Russell girlfriend, who was less than pleased about his antics and in a huff with him for the rest of the day. By the morning she had thawed and they were the best of friends again, staying close to each other's side. It was as though Crumpet wouldn't let Marmite out of her sight in case he managed to get himself into even more mischief!

The rescue story didn't end there. Somehow the newspapers heard about it and Nikki was called for interviews and asked to pose with Marmite for photographs at the entrance of the shaft. Later she learned the fire brigade had sent out a press release. Suddenly, Marmite was a celebrity and his face was on the TV news. He was part of a rescue reconstruction with the fire brigade buddies who had hauled him out. Then the papers got wind of it and he was in the *Telegraph*, the *Guardian*, the *Daily Mirror* and the *Sun*.

He was also under a new regime. Nikki was taking him on daily walks and insisting he was on a long lead whenever he was out in the yard. So he had some freedom, but not so much that he could run off when he fancied a bit of excitement.

A year later, he became a father, probably passing his 'survival' genes to the next generation.

❧ Crumpet ❧

For all the press coverage that was spun from Marmite's miraculous rescue, there was one story that the papers and TV crews failed to pick up. This wasn't his first time as escape artist *extraordinaire* and there was another dog hero in their presence, in fact a dog *heroine*, Crumpet herself.

Marmite had first gone missing exactly a year earlier. Finding him hadn't been easy because the sand quarry right next to Nikki's house is so huge it makes tracking a dog like finding a flea in an Afghan hound. Every day Nikki had taken Crumpet out with her, hoping her keen sense of smell could help in the search, but she would either look uninterested or chase rabbit scents, scattering the search team, who would dig holes wherever she ran in the vague hope of digging up Marmite.

After a week of digging without any sign, Nikki did a web search looking for help. Like many people she hadn't heard of animal communication, but she was willing to give it a try. After all, she'd already tried search and rescue dogs, hunt terriers, a bloodhound, mini diggers and a huge JCB digger.

I communicated distantly with Marmite and passed on to Nikki the details he gave me: trapped in sand, rabbit hole, red brick and canal lock. Nikki was puzzled by this, as she informed me there was no brick anywhere on the quarry.

After two days of searching the old buildings of a neighbouring farm and various other locations, Nikki came across an area that seemed to match Marmite's description. Crumpet's barking was different at this location and even the German Shepherd who was with Nikki began to get animated for the first time. Before she'd even had time to feel doubtful, Crumpet reacted like a doggie possessed: she dug and dug and dug, sending sand flying until her paws began to bleed. Still she wouldn't stop. She continued to kick sand until she had disappeared from view. Minutes went by, which dragged on like hours for those waiting above. The search party stood outside the hole, speechless and worried, but with hope building.

All of a sudden Crumpet popped out, plastered in orange sand, hardly able to see. Then out from another hole beside her came another tail, and a thin, tired, orange little dog clambered out: Marmite. He was alive! Screams and cheers filled the air and Marmite was scooped up for a hug. He'd survived seven nights trapped down a rabbit hole with no food, no water and barely enough air to breathe. Just as he'd explained, the hole had caved in on him and he'd found himself underground, facing the wrong way and buried under a mountain of sand. But Crumpet had managed to dig him free.

There were no film crews waiting to immortalize this life-saving moment, no journalists queuing for interviews and no photo shoot for the local papers, but Nikki and Marmite knew that Crumpet was a true heroine.

A nice headline could have been 'Crumpet Saves Marmite So They Can Toast Together.'

CHAPTER 16

Tracking 'Miracle' Alfie

ONLY 15 DAYS after I'd helped find Marmite, I had a request to track another missing Jack Russell. Patterns seem to emerge like this. One week I'll receive a handful of horse communications, then I'll be swamped in Burmese cats and another time it will be bunny week. Sometimes I'll receive a variety of species but they'll all be the same colour.

Pamela e-mailed: 'Alfie has been missing for three days and has never been out overnight before. He is a very loving dog and will sometimes wake me up in the night just for a cuddle.'

She told me he had last been seen when she, her husband, her two children and Alfie's sister Katie had all gone for a walk on Telegraph Hill in Surrey. Both Jack Russells had taken off as soon as they had been let off the lead. The last sight Pamela had of them was a flash of white paws sprinting into Hinchley Wood. They didn't reappear and Pamela's husband had been searching all day, covering as much of the wood as possible. He hadn't been able to find them, but Katie knew the mile-long route home and had walked back under her own steam later that evening, covered in sand with really sore front paws. Pamela imagined this was from digging.

Her e-mail continued:

Katie and Alfie have been together ever since they were born. Katie is generally the naughty one with a real gleam in her eye and she likes to pretend that she is the boss, but Alfie is the one who is really in charge. We often walk them in the park by the river at East Molesey and when we turn back to the car park Katie will catch Alfie's eye and the two of them will run off into the trees to chase squirrels. Generally we try and get Alfie on the lead before she catches his eye!

They are great at catching mice and make a really impressive team. Katie does the chasing and then there's one blow from Alfie and it's curtains.

They have run off before and in the past Alfie has been the one who has always come back first. My greatest fear is that he is buried somewhere and cannot get home. His sister misses him and we desperately need to know what has happened to him.

I had two days of clients' cases and commitments before I was finally able to look at the photo of Alfie and begin communicating. It was now four nights and five days since he'd disappeared. As I looked at his photo I could see a Jack Russell with a difference: curly beige and white hair framed his face, giving him a very soft, noble air. I imagined him to be a French marquis or adventurous musketeer. His gentle eyes shone with love and his black button nose added to his friendly and approachable demeanour. The moment we connected I could feel he was very gentle but also a lot of fun. He showed me images of bone-shaped crunchy biscuits and I heard little yaps of excitement. He showed a picture of himself play fighting with Katie on a rug. He came across as a really sweet guy.

Having a sense that time was not on our side, I got straight to the important questions. 'How are you, Alfie?' I said.

'Can't breathe,' came the reply.

'Where are you?' I said, concerned.

He showed me an image of earth and then himself beneath the earth's surface.

'Are you trapped underground?' I checked.

I saw an image of Alfie and then soil falling down on him, tightly encasing him under its heavy weight. Pamela's greatest fear appeared to be true.

'Are you still in Hinchley Wood?' I said, holding my breath as I waited.

'Yes,' he said, calmly.

Exhaling with relief, I said, 'What happened?'

'She followed me in. I went first. The same hole,' he replied.

'Both you and Katie went down the same hole?'

He replied with a note of excitement, 'Yes. Badger scent.'

He showed me the image again: his small body surrounded by soil, his head facing inwards and his bottom closest to the surface.

'Can't you turn round?' I said.

'No,' he replied sadly, and I felt a sinking feeling in my chest.

I moved my awareness into his body. Immediately the air quality was suffocating. It felt as though I was inhaling soil rather than air. The taste seemed to smother my tongue and my throat. I felt cramped – Alfie couldn't move.

'You're going to be all right,' I said, then moved my awareness out of his body and back into my own.

I now realized Alfie was trapped and weak and we needed to get him out quickly. As an animal communicator, having empathy for distressed animals is crucial, but the thing that is really needed is to be in a calm space. Instead of adding to the drama of their distress by becoming distressed ourselves, we can be the calm, supportive influence that soothes their fears.

'I need to know where to find you,' I said. 'Can you show me what it looks like above you?'

I saw an open grassy area, then Alfie and his sister running into the woods together, excited and focused. The floor of the wood was covered in brown leaves and the trees were very tall with trunks about a foot wide. I didn't know what type they were but I could see a lot of trunk before the branches began. Even though there were a lot of trees, daylight was able to cut through the branches. *Right, that sounds like any other wood, but let's keep going,* I thought.

'Do you remember what the entrance to the hole was like?' I said to Alfie silently in my mind, and he showed me brambles and overgrowth.

The problem was that in a wood full of brambles and overgrowth he could be anywhere. With time running out I needed something more specific. I decided I needed to hone down a spot.

'Can you show me the whole area again?' I said. This time I was looking for landmarks, something that would stand out to Pamela.

An image came into my mind. From my point of view the wood was directly in front of me and there was a wooden bench over to the right, which stood on flat grass. The grass sloped away in front of the bench and also to the right of it. Then the image switched to black compressed soil, confirming my feeling that Alfie was literally buried alive, his body wedged in one of the holes by lots of earth. I felt Pamela and I needed to act fast to save him.

'Can you hear Pamela calling you? Or any of the family?' I said, concerned but calm.

He let me sense that it was silent; he couldn't hear anything.

Thinking on my feet, I zoomed my awareness outwards so I could take in the whole wood. It appeared almost square but with rounded edges. I tried something new and mentally divided the area into four equal parts. 'Which part are you in?' I said to Alfie, while keeping the image in my mind. He showed me the bottom left section. Little did I know that this grid work would become a regular part of my practice.

'And whereabouts in this section?' I said, knowing it was still a large area and that I needed to push for even greater detail.

He pictured himself almost at the centre of the section but slightly over to the upper right.

I hoped I'd now gathered enough detail. I immediately typed up some impressions of Alfie's character and e-mailed them to Pamela. I wanted us both to be sure I was connected to him before I revealed my findings. Within an hour she had replied positively and we'd arranged an immediate phone call.

On the phone, I went through a steady process of revealing details and waiting to see if Pamela confirmed them. Knowing that the guardian of a missing animal is upset and emotional, I like to try and calm them down and bring their focus to every impression in a slow, measured way. It would be easy to blurt out what I've received, but that would be a mistake. Often I repeat details twice to be sure the guardian is confirming them, otherwise we might both follow a line of enquiry which could waste valuable search time.

When I described what I visualized as Telegraph Hill, the wooded area, the bench positioned in front of the trees and the grass sloping away, Pamela said, 'That's the bench where my children sat while my husband was trying to find Alfie and Katie.'

'It's on flat grass, slightly to the right, and the grass slopes away in front of it and on its right side – is that right?' I wanted to confirm.

'Sorry, say that again so I can picture it,' Pamela said.

'Imagine yourself sitting on the bench where your children sat. The ground slopes away to the left and the wooded area is behind you. Does that make sense?'

'Yes!' she said, excitement building.

'OK, let me tell you what I feel from my communication with Alfie,' I said, trying to calm her with the tone of my voice.

'OK,' she replied.

'I feel Alfie is still alive.'

'Thank goodness,' Pamela interjected, before I'd a chance to finish.

'I'm sorry, it's not all good news. I feel he's underground, trapped down a hole, and it appears that the earth has caved in on him, which is why he hasn't been able to get out.'

'That's been our worry. My husband has searched for hours all over that wood, digging and calling for him,' she said, resigned.

'I feel it's silent where he is. He can't hear you calling for him, but he's feeling calm,' I told her.

'How can I find him? It's such a huge area.'

'I'm going to give you an image to help you. You may want to draw it. Have you got a piece of paper?' I said.

When Pamela was ready I asked her to draw a square, divide it into four equal sections and then put a dot in the centre of the bottom left square. 'This is the layout of the wood if I'm picturing myself standing facing it. So the bench is positioned close to the wood and slightly over to the right. I feel he's close to this dot, but slightly further up and over to the right,' I said.

Pamela immediately recognized this area, 'But that's where we've been looking! We were digging there a few days ago. We gave up because Katie didn't react. How can I find Alfie if he can't hear me calling him?'

'If you can go back out and call him again, I'll talk to him and encourage him to dig. I'll explain to him that he's not going to get out unless he can help you reach him,' I told her. I also suggested she hire someone with thermal imaging equipment. Then we ended our call.

I looked at Alfie's photo again and went back into communication with him: 'Alfie, Pamela is on her way out to you right now, but you're going to have to dig, sweetheart. It's going to be hard to find you, so you need to start digging yourself back to the surface. I know you can do it.'

Then, to make it perfectly clear, I gave him a picture image of what I wanted him to do.

About an hour later my phone rang.

'I've got him. He's alive,' Pamela told me with classic English reserve.

'Is he OK?' I replied.

'Yes, he's all right. Covered in soil.'

I was thrilled to bits.

Later, once the shock had worn off, Pamela shared the whole story:

After your call, I phoned a friend in tears and she said she would come to the woods with me. I took a garden hoe and Katie on her lead and we went back to the place you'd described, which is where my husband had been digging. While we were waiting for the thermal imaging guy I'd hired, I began trying to clear the entrance to the hole so that he would be able to get his equipment into it. Katie was completely uninterested in the hole and more focused on the squirrels in the trees above.

After a few minutes, I stopped scraping the earth and said to my friend, 'This is completely useless. We're never going to find him.'

Just then she said, 'Pamela, look – the earth is moving.'

The earth was moving to the side of the hole entrance and then a little white paw burst through the earth and Katie began to go crazy, digging. I was so excited I just pulled the paw as hard as I could, and out came Alfie, straight out of the ground.

He was so excited to be free. Instead of appearing tired and weak, he ran around in circles. Katie sniffed him, but then got really annoyed with him and decided to tell him off by biting him!

I had been so despondent I hadn't even thought to take his lead with me. We had to put him on the lead with Katie.

I rang my husband but couldn't speak for crying. I eventually managed to sob, 'I've got him!'

On the way back home we called into the vet's and made an appointment to get him checked over. He has lost a kilo and is very dehydrated, but other than that he is fine.

I still can't quite believe our luck. Alfie's our 'miracle' dog. He is being treated like a king – nothing but freshly cooked chicken or his favourite meaty dog food until he gains his kilo back. I was very surprised to find him asleep under the bed on his first night home. After his ordeal I would have thought he wouldn't want to be hemmed in, but then he always has slept under there so it's home to him.

How is it possible for a dog to live entombed in soil without water for four nights and five days? I feel Alfie saved his own life, with the help of our connection. When animals feel defeated and down, a bit of love and encouragement can be enough to spur them on. Through my instructions and encouragement Alfie found the strength to get out of his hole, and he did it by himself. I don't know how he turned round, but I don't need to. What's important to me is that he survived. And at barely four years old, he still has the rest of his life ahead of him.

CHAPTER 17

King Curtis and Big Love

CURTIS IS A DOG I think of with fondness in my heart. I
first met him when Mark, his guardian, e-mailed to arrange
an in-person consultation with him. Curtis was a rescued dog
who had been badly treated for most of his six years until a
neighbour had stolen him away from his abusive situation, and
then he had been passed on from one person to another and
then another. When Mark heard he was about to be given to
the dogs' home, he stepped in and took him home. He was his
first dog and was originally called Snoopy, but he was not a
Snoopy. A couple of years earlier Mark and his wife, Sue, had
seen a bar sign, 'King Curtis', and had agreed that if they ever
had a dog, that's what he would be called. And King Curtis he
was.

Mark wrote:

There he was, my future best friend, just waiting for me at
Clapham Junction station, neglected and overlooked, passed
around by too many people who could never appreciate what an

incredible being they had in their midst. I know he was waiting for us, and for that I am eternally grateful.

So, on 14 August 2006, there I was ringing a doorbell in London Bridge. I'd asked for the usual information: Curtis's breed, age, photo, how long he'd been with his guardian and up to 10 questions or messages. I'd already communicated distantly with Curtis himself ahead of the home visit. So it was reassuring to be met by Mark, who had dark hair, and to be taken up in a lift to the fifth floor, just as Curtis had described to me. Curtis had also pictured his home as an open-plan living-room, kitchen and dining-room with an expansive floor-to-ceiling glass front overlooking a grassy area. As Mark took me from the lift into his flat I found myself standing in the open-plan flat Curtis had shown me. One of Mark's concerns was Curtis's comprehension, but from the evidence so far, he seemed to be as sharp as the eyes of a hawk.

Curtis slowly walked over to greet me and as I bent down to say hello, I looked into his eyes and my heart leapt. With that one glance I could see the wise old soul that was his real self. He stood there in his bony whippet-like Staffordshire cross body with greying black wiry hair and a white blaze down his chest. I loved the distinguished grey heart shaping his chocolate coloured eyes, which were shining with intelligence. He really was very striking and his energetic presence more than made up for his physical fragility; he was now 18 years old.

Mark, his attractive and petite wife Sue and I settled on the floor cushions around Curtis and began the consultation.

'Is Curtis happy with us?' they said.

I referred to my notebook and read out what he'd said during our distant communication: 'Oh yes! I love being with them. They are so much fun.'

Mark and Sue were smiling. 'That's what we thought,' Mark said, 'but we wanted to still ask him, because he doesn't give much away these days.'

Mark told me Curtis was showing signs of senility: he'd forget where he was, get stuck behind furniture, be confused by familiar things and stare blankly. During my visit I could see that – he'd wander off, occasionally getting stuck between the kitchen units, or he'd stand with a vacant look on his face. Sue would go to him and gently bring him back and we'd see his spirit reappear behind his eyes.

'Is he happy within himself?' Mark said.

'I wouldn't want to be anywhere else,' Curtis responded, 'but I feel achy, creaky. My back and hips …' It was as though he was reading a shopping list.

I told Mark and Sue what he'd communicated and also that I felt he had some mild heart irregularity, hip dysplasia and arthritic joints.

'Yes, he's got lots going on, all of that, and he's on medication from the vet, but he seems OK with it and we just do whatever we have to do to make sure he's comfortable. He's been having seizures on and off for several years,' said Mark, in a gentle tone. I could see the love pouring out of him whenever he spoke of Curtis. 'Is there anything else we can do for him that we're not already doing, or is there anything he wishes we would do differently?'

'Lots of fish. Love sardines. I love food. They try to get me to eat a bland, boring diet,' I heard Curtis say, laughing.

'He said that? I don't believe him!' said Sue, now laughing too. 'Curtis eats the best of everything. I work in the food industry and he often has leftovers from my photo shoots – organic steak, chicken, cheese, you name it! – but if there's something he wants instead then we'll get it for him.'

'I think he must be having a joke,' I replied. 'I felt there was something not quite right about his answer. He said it with a smile in his voice.'

This is one of the problems with telepathy, which leaves the animal communicator to explain that although the communication appears wrong, it's only because the animal is taking the mickey. All animals can have a sense of humour; it's not an exclusive human quality.

Mark and Sue were both laughing now, and when I looked over to Curtis, even though his face was fixed in its usual expressionless pose, I sensed him grinning inside.

'Curtis pictures himself on the sofa, I think watching TV,' I said. 'Sue, you're on his left, and Mark, you're on his right. He's giving me the feeling he loves to be on the sofa between you.'

'Oh good, we love that too. We often sit with Curtis between us watching TV. That's just how we like it,' said Mark, smiling, then he moved on to the next question. 'His behaviour has changed over the past year, as he's become older, and we'd like to know if he's happy with some of the changes he's made?'

'He says he finds it harder to walk about and he gets very stiff,' I explained.

'Oh, Curtis, we know. We're sorry you're feeling stiff. We're always happy to walk at his pace so he doesn't need to rush,' said Mark, softly stroking Curtis, who was lying by his leg. 'Does he still like going for a longer walk in the park or does he prefer the shorter walk in our neighbourhood park?'

'He says he likes lots of short walks in the park with the kids' playground. The one close by.'

'I like hearing children laugh,' Curtis added.

That reminded me of a TV programme where someone explained that adults tend to laugh approximately 17 times a day but children can laugh around 300 times.

'We walk him in that park,' Mark said, pointing at a small one visible from their balcony. 'There is a playground and also a tennis court, and sometimes kids go in there to kick a ball about.'

'We like to vary his walks,' explained Sue, 'but we do walk him in there quite a lot and he gets to meet all his dog friends. It's become a place to meet other people out with their dog and have a chat.'

'Some of Curtis's behavioural changes aren't a problem, but what is happening now is that he has a tendency to urinate in the house in the evenings unless we take him out for frequent walks, which he doesn't need during the day or through the night. Does he indicate any reason for urinating inside during the evening?'

Curtis gave three short answers: 'You're not always here. My bladder gets full. You are relaxing.'

Later Mark said, 'That was one of the most significant things you ever told me about Curtis. I distinctly remember talking to Sue about it after the communication. Until that moment I had no idea a dog could understand the nuances of our behaviour so perceptively. I get it now of course, but until then it had never occurred to me that animals could read us so well, that they could understand our moods beyond the obvious and that they could put our needs before their own just to make us happy. Curtis taught us that and I'll never forget it.'

'It seems he doesn't want to disturb you,' I explained, 'but he doesn't say why he can then hold his bladder all through the night. I've asked him to go to the front door next time, so you have a sign that he needs to go out.'

'Does he like being looked after by Sue's parents?' Mark said.

'I love them,' Curtis immediately replied, 'young at heart, lots of fun. They give me lots of love and just let me be. They are easy-going and caring, just like Sue.'

Mark and Sue told me Sue's parents hadn't been too keen on them getting a dog because they had been concerned about the pain that falling in love with a dog can bring once he is no longer with you. However, on meeting Curtis they had absolutely fallen in love with him.

'If Mark ever asks them about it now,' Sue said, 'they conveniently forget that they ever suggested we shouldn't get a dog. In fact they claim they encouraged us!'

'Above all, we wish Curtis to know that we love him and want him to be happy and that we'll do whatever we can to make sure he's safe and content,' Mark said.

'He's happy. He adores you both,' I said, to put their minds at rest.

At the end of the consultation we said our goodbyes and I left Curtis to the hugs and kisses of his adoring guardians.

On 14 December, exactly six months later, I was connecting with Curtis again, distantly, using his photo, but this time he wasn't cheeky and joking, he was tired and contemplative. Mark and Sue were both worried because he was struggling with his daily routine. He had also begun to pee in their bedroom and they wondered if he was trying to tell them something.

'It's nearly time to go,' he got in first.

'Do you know how soon?' I said.

'Maybe three weeks, 3 January,' he replied.

'Are you sure?' I said, knowing full well I shouldn't really question an animal's response, but it was such a huge concern.

'I am so tired of being ill, of feeling this way,' he replied. 'It will only get worse and I want my grace and dignity. It's time.'

Later I looked 3 January up in my diary and realized it was exactly three weeks from the day of that communication.

On the last visit we'd agreed that Curtis would lie down in the hallway, where he never lay normally, if he needed help to pass.

'I want one more Christmas,' he continued, 'I am making the most of my final days. It's been a long life. I cannot keep going forever.'

'OK, sweetheart, I'll tell them. Can I ask you one more thing? They wish to know why you're peeing in their bedroom.'

'Because I'm too scared to go onto the balcony,' he replied, and then I saw the balcony the way he saw it, very dim and hard to distinguish. It would make sense that he'd toilet where he felt safe, in the place that smelled strongly of his guardians.

'Tell them I love them,' he continued, 'but to love we have to let go of the very thing we hold tightly to our hearts. It is a great love, a love that takes courage, unconditional love, *big love*.'

I typed up Curtis's communication and e-mailed it to Mark and Sue, but I excluded the time frame and date he'd given. Understandably, they were devastated, but Mark wrote back, 'Above all I want what's right for Curtis and we'll do whatever we have to in order to make it as easy and as comfortable for him as possible. We just have to be as brave as he is.'

Curtis added one more comment he wanted me to pass on to Mark and I e-mailed it over:

He talked about Christmas and wanted to check the arrangements! Will you have a tree up, in the dining area, with bright lights and pretty coloured baubles? He pictured purple baubles. He really would like a bright, colourful Christmas with lots of happiness from you guys, doing what you like to do the most. He would like to see you really having a happy time. All this would make him feel very happy.

Mark replied:

> We do indeed have purple baubles; in fact that's the only colour
> we have on the tree, other than white or silver. I could barely
> remember that – I can't believe Curtis does! We weren't going to
> put the tree up until the eighteenth, as Sue will be away until
> then, but if he's looking forward to a tree then we'll put it up this
> weekend before she leaves. We're really looking forward to
> Christmas, it's a nice quiet time for us and it means we can really
> relax.

Then Mark asked me to tell him the date Curtis had given for
his ascension.

I wrote back:

> I can't tell you how concerned I am about telling you the date I felt
> Curtis gave me. My worry is that I may have it wrong and will let
> you all down, but on the other hand I also feel Curtis wouldn't
> give a date without a reason. Maybe he is preparing you for when
> he won't be there, a bit like advance notice so you can come to
> terms with losing him. It sounds as though he is also making it
> easier on you both, taking the decision and responsibility away
> from you, as he would. After he said, 'It is nearly time to go,' I
> asked him how long and he replied, 'Three weeks. On 3 January.'

After that, Mark and Sue were determined to make this the
best Christmas ever for Curtis. I connected with him again on
2 January and he showed a picture of himself being really

quite sprightly at home with a big smile on his face. He had just loved Christmas and seemed far from ready to ascend. I wrote to Mark and Sue to give them these details and to remind them to listen to their hearts and their own knowing, rather than sticking with the date I'd received. Crucially, Curtis hadn't given the agreed sign.

Mark and Sue were already consulting their own vet, but they had decided that the final decision-maker would be Curtis himself.

On 4 January I received news from Mark:

> Yesterday came and went without a sign from Curtis, so we're not going to do anything until he either gives us the sign or things get worse for him physically. He's such a tough old guy, I think he's just decided he's not that bad at the moment and might as well stay around while things are good – either that or he's being really cheeky by telling us he's planning on passing over just so he can get some extra-special food and walks!

I was so glad they'd listened to their hearts rather than accept the date as fixed. I know that animals, like people, change their minds. The heart always has a clearer feeling.

I did some further communication with Curtis. He said, 'Both their love and the extra company saw me through Christmas. I was much happier.'

Mark and Sue's love saw Curtis go on way beyond that. At the end of March, Mark reported that his health was getting worse and asked, 'Is there anything he's looking forward to now? Is there something on a regular basis that keeps him happy?'

'Your company keeps me happy. Otherwise there is nothing. Day in, day out I struggle,' Curtis said, with both love and resignation in his voice.

'We're going away for four days at the end of April,' Mark said. 'Is there anything we can do to help him relax about this? Sue's parents will be staying at our place to look after him.'

'Don't go. Don't go,' Curtis said, 'I don't want you to leave me. You promised. Or take me too. We need to be together. I need to be with you.' Then I felt feelings of sadness and anxiety, as he said, 'But you have made up your minds already.'

'Oh, we didn't know he felt like this. I'll talk to Sue about it,' Mark said. 'Overall, is he happy to keep going as is?'

'I can't see a way out,' Curtis said simply.

I reminded him he could give Mark and Sue the signal if he was ready to go, but he said he wasn't. He knew he wouldn't feel their touch again and he would miss that the most. So he wanted to stay for as long as possible.

Mark ended the communication by asking me to pass a message to Curtis: 'We just want him to know that we love him, that we're happy for him to be with us as long as he wants and that we'll support whatever decision he wants to make.'

The strength Curtis's guardians mustered as they faced the experience of his death is a lesson in courage all of us could draw upon. Animal communication with him, as with many other animals, helped his guardians lessen their fear of the end of his life as they focused on what was right for him.

One thing they did was to change their holiday from Spain to Cornwall, so that they could take him with them. When they returned, they contacted me:

The sun shone, the air was warm, the days were beautiful and we spent as much time with Curtis by the sea as possible. He was so peaceful, it was incredible. At night he'd curl up with me by the fire in a way he's never done at any other time. It's hard to describe, but it was total and utter contentment beyond anything I'd seen before. He did have a few seizures during the week. As you know, throughout his life he's suffered from mild epilepsy, but this week it was different, especially on the drive home. We were concerned when we left; I don't know if we're misinterpreting this, but it seemed that he didn't want to leave. On Friday he vomited just before we set off and then he had three big seizures on the trip back and each time we thought we were going to lose him. And another thing that's odd is that he refused to urinate on the way home, despite us stopping every 90 minutes to try. It wasn't until 3.30 in the morning that he peed again – a full 15 hours since getting in the car! Even in his younger days he wouldn't go 15 hours. What makes it harder, too, is that he just keeps getting slower and more tired all the time, so it's more and more difficult for us to determine what's really going on. Poor thing, his spirit is just sooo much stronger than his frail little body, we're just watching him visibly wind down every day.

I asked distantly again.

'Hi there, Curtis,' I said, once I'd connected with him, 'how are you?'

'I just feel stuck. I want to go now,' he said sadly. 'That was our last holiday and I *loved* the holiday. I just wanted one last special time to feel the sea, just the three of us, like it used to be. I love them so much, so very, very much. I will never leave them because they are in my heart. Eventually they will learn this. They are very loving, *fun* people. I have loved the fun with them. Now I can't bear it anymore. I am letting go, that's why I am having so many seizures. It's time, Pea. I need their help.'

I felt upset to hear his reply. 'Did you enjoy the holiday?' I said, trying to remain calm.

'It was the best holiday, the best time. Just what I wanted.'

'Why did you go 15 hours without urinating?'

'So they would contact you,' he replied.

I found the words hard to read back to Mark, but he found them harder to hear and often went quiet. Mark and Sue were the most loving, caring and thoughtful guardians any dog could ever wish to have and now they started to make the arrangements so Curtis's passing could be as calm and beautiful as possible. Curtis had communicated that he would be happy to be at home and he asked for Mark to hold him in his arms as he ascended. He wanted to be as close to him as possible. Mark asked me to join them to offer Curtis support in his final moments in this lifetime and to relay any last messages or requests he might make.

On 15 May I took the London Underground to their flat. On the way I reached out energetically to connect with Curtis to reassure him he'd be gently released from his body soon. He wasn't worried, but he asked me to do him an important favour. That's how I found myself calling into a florist's on the way. Minutes later I was inside Mark and Sue's flat holding two large deep red roses, one for Sue and one for Mark. 'These are a gift from Curtis, a token of his love for you both. To remind you he will always be with you in your heart. He asked me to bring them,' I said, handing the roses to Sue.

She took me out to the balcony where Mark was sitting, holding Curtis on the new lime-green UFO-style sofa seat purchased especially for 'hugging Curtis' moments. Curtis was lying on his side in Mark's arms, dozing. Mark was astonished that, yet again, despite Curtis's physical condition, he had the courage and the consideration to put their feelings before his own. 'What an amazing soul he is to have thought of us that way and to be looking out for us until the very end,' he said, clearly surprised.

I could see how tired Curtis was now. He'd been expressing how tired he was getting, but because he always communicated with such a strong spirit it was hard to fully comprehend. Now I could see with my own eyes that he was at the end of his journey. As I gently stroked his bony arms and skinny body, I said, 'How are you, Curtis?'

'Ready,' he replied calmly, his peaceful eyes looking back at me. It was the right time, on the right day.

Mark and Sue wanted to make Curtis's ascension a celebration of his life rather than a grim, miserable affair. Sue came out with glasses of wine and we toasted Curtis and they talked over his cheeky antics and the hotels he'd frequented across the world. It seemed that he wasn't just a London boy, he was a globetrotter. He had crossed the Atlantic twice and had been everywhere from New York to New Orleans. He had also managed to procure a room upgrade on more than one occasion. Mark and Sue had been upgraded to a diplomat's suite at the Watergate in Washington, DC, because of him. In Ottawa at the Fairmont Château Laurier they had been put in a club room because he had made such an impression, and in Manhattan, at the Alex, when they had had to wait as their room wasn't quite ready, after 10 minutes or so in the lobby Curtis had decided to bark in frustration and within seconds the porter had come over and told them he could have a room ready immediately – an upgrade, of course.

One of the funniest moments in travelling with Curtis was when they had all arrived at the Charleston Place Hotel in South Carolina, which at the time was ranked as the fourth best hotel in all of America, and he had jumped out of the car and run in circles around the concièrge's desk in absolute delight. Rolling their eyes, Mark and Sue had run into the lobby to retrieve him, but he had brought nothing but laughter to the staff, who all thought he was the 'sweetest thang'.

No matter where they had gone with him, Curtis had taken good weather along – every single time. In North America they had always had fantastic weather, no matter where they went, and not just in obvious places either. They had record heat for Christmas in New Orleans, perfect snow in Vermont over another Christmas and a gorgeous new year in New York. In the UK Curtis always brought them the best as well, giving them freakishly warm temperatures in Cornwall in September, despite rain just before their arrival and again just after. And should they dare to take a trip without him, to Spain for instance, it would simply rain. Mark didn't know how scientific it was, but declared Curtis certainly had *the weather mojo*.

But that was all in the past. Now the vet was stuck in traffic and Curtis was growing impatient with her. 'She said six o'clock, where is she?' he said.

'I'm sorry, Curtis, she's stuck in traffic,' I explained. 'Is there anything you'd like while we're waiting?'

'Some more chicken please. Now.'

Mark lifted him into the kitchen, where he hand-fed him his final supper. Sue showed me the candles they had burning especially for him, honouring his life, and she put on some relaxing music that she thought he would find soothing. I was touched by these details. The music was a mix of chill-out tracks that they'd both loved over the years and things they'd enjoyed together on road trips and holidays – 'A Grand Love Theme' by Kid Loco, 'Star' by Primal Scream, 'Sunworshipper' by Mylo (King Curtis loved the sun) and 'La Femme d'Argent' by Air (according to Mark, one of the most beautiful songs ever recorded). These were standout tracks that had some resonance for them no matter where they were or what they were doing, and Curtis had always been a big part of those times.

It wasn't long before the doorbell rang and Mark and Sue gathered Curtis up in their arms and took him into their bedroom to say their final goodbyes.

'This is going to be hard, isn't it?' the vet said to me, as she prepared the needles.

'No, it will be fine. Curtis is ready to go and they are ready to let him go,' I replied.

Mark carried Curtis back into the room and settled down on one of the large floor cushions with Curtis on his lap, hugging him to his chest. Sue seemed lost and didn't know what to do, so I gently encouraged her to be close to Mark and Curtis.

The room was so peaceful. The vet asked whether Mark and Sue were ready and they said they were. I also heard Curtis respond, 'Yes.' Mark remained so strong and brave as the vet inserted the first needle into Curtis's leg and pushed in the sedative. Then he spoke softly to Curtis, 'We know it's time for you to go. We're being strong for you just as you asked. It's OK for you to go now, we understand, and no matter how sad it makes us feel, we want to do what's right for you, because we love you and you've been the best dog ever.'

Time seemed to stop still while we all waited for the sedative to do its work and the flat seemed to grow even quieter. Then the vet inserted the second needle and Curtis was given the final dose that would relieve him of his pain, his indignity, seizures and suffering. The instant the needle was in I saw a grey almost transparent wisp begin exiting his body from his chest area. I watched it until it had completely left his body and was floating up and away from him. It vanished a foot or so above his head. Tears silently ran down my face.

Mark continued looking at Curtis as he held him tight, soothing him with loving words. 'Has he gone?' he said to the vet, tears pouring down his face.

'No, not yet,' she said, after putting her stethoscope up to his heart, 'a little longer.' She didn't know Curtis's spirit had already left. His heart may have had a few more beats to express, but he was free now.

We continued to sit still a little longer, with Curtis's body wrapped inside Mark's arms. Then his head rolled onto Mark's chest and there was an exhalation of air as his lungs emptied. The vet listened for his heartbeat again and this time she confirmed he had gone. Mark and Sue held him for a while, then wrapped a blanket gently round his worn-out body, which they lowered into a wicker basket the vet had brought with her.

We all went out to the vet's car. Mark carried the basket and then placed it gently onto the back seat. The vet's friendly dog was in the car and it felt somehow right that he was sitting beside the basket, working with his mum as she eased animals' suffering. She'd been very sensitive to Mark and Sue's emotions and had prepared thoughtful details like the blanket and basket. As she drove away, Mark, Sue and I exchanged hugs and said goodbye.

Mark later wrote about his experience of animal communication with Curtis. Here is his side of the story:

It wasn't that we weren't prepared to accept communication was genuinely possible, but I had trouble with certain aspects of it that I didn't understand and it took me a while to get over those doubts. After experience, research and observation, however, it suddenly made sense and I realized what an utterly incredible thing it was, sitting there right under all of our noses and most of us oblivious to it.

We knew Curtis well and we had a wonderful life together, but we were never open enough to listen to the things he said. Until the communications with Pea we never knew the details – and the details made the difference in the end. It wasn't just that he was clear in his messages, it was his sense of humour that was most surprising – in fact I always said to Pea that I often laughed at many of the things Curtis *did* but I never imagined that I would be laughing at the things he *said*.

It goes without saying that his passing was an emotional moment, and one that we second-guessed right up to the end. How could we possibly let him go? He was clearly nearing the end of his physical life, but at the same time, how could we go ahead with it? When he finally went, I was holding him and his body felt so different – it's a strange sensation, after you've been so used to another being's physical presence to have it change so dramatically, but it did help to underline that he really had gone.

Looking back now, we have no doubts and no regrets. That's not to say it makes it any easier in the moment – it's still heart-wrenching – but the knowledge of someone's readiness to go does change your perspective entirely and provides a framework for the final act. To see the look on his face while I held him on our balcony before the vet arrived was to see true tranquillity. I've never before or since seen such utter – well, *peace*, for want of a better word. He was absolutely, truly and utterly content.

The first night and the first day without Curtis were just strange. We endured of course – there's nothing more that you can do. We were fortunate to have someone like Pea bridge the gap that most people can't overcome, to give us the insight that we don't have (but should) and to make what is such a difficult time into something that can be remembered (albeit with tears) as something that was dignified, courteous and respectful. I can't downplay Pea's role in it – without her involvement we wouldn't have the same peace about Curtis's final days that we do and we wouldn't have the understanding that we were *really* doing the right thing for him, and that's something that makes you understand how truly insightful animals are.

During a communication with Curtis after he'd passed, he gave Pea the image of him being carried around Tanner Street Park in a sedan chair! He also promoted himself from King to Emperor! Cheeky monkey (although I can think of no one more deserving).

The last thing I asked Pea to tell Curtis was I felt he had changed my life. Curtis, big joker that he is, and sage of sages at the same time, suddenly changed his tone and humbly told Pea that *we* had changed *his* life too. This touched my heart beyond description. If I've done nothing else in my life, that's why I've been here, to hear something like that.

Curtis was such an inspiration to us and to others in the way that he soldiered on – but that doesn't mean we don't remember him as his true self, all vibrant and happy and full of life, because that's what I do think of now when I picture him in my mind, laughing and smiling and barking with glee. It's funny when we look at pictures of him, because for a dog that was generally aloof with people (Curtis didn't come to you, *you* went to Curtis) we have *loads* of photos of him with the biggest, happiest grin on his face you can imagine.

Pea Horsley

It has to be the greatest honour of my work as an animal communicator to offer my support to both an animal and the guardians at the heartbreaking time when it comes to say goodbye. To love and let go, as Mark and Sue did, is, as Curtis himself said, 'a great love, a love that takes courage, unconditional love, *big love*'.

CHAPTER 18

Love

DURING THE YEARS I have been communicating with animals I have heard many wonderful stories. The underlying theme is always the same: love, pure and uncomplicated. Animals do not judge us like humans do. They don't care if we look like a catwalk model or the dog's dinner. They certainly don't care about the size of our bank account or our occupational status. Their love is unconditional, because for them love is simple.

Morgan would rather I am in the moment 'being' with him than listening to my iPod or talking on my mobile, and Texas would prefer me to offer him a warm lap and gaze lovingly into his eyes than racing around panicking about everything that needs to be done. They both prefer sharing a sacred moment in time together, where our hearts are connected. These are special times indeed – the essence of love. When our companions are long gone and we are left behind, these are the precious moments we will remember – the cuddles, the joyful walks and the sitting in silence together.

Without a doubt animals are fabulous teachers. Some of their lessons can soothe us and sometimes they challenge us to grow beyond our current experience.

❧ *Bonnie Speaks Her Loving Truth* ❧

I love feisty animals. Bonnie, a 20-year-old jet-black kick-arse cat, is one of my favourites. Every communication I've had with her has been an enlightening experience.

Bonnie has been sick with a handful of concerns over a number of years – a thyroid tumour, blood pressure, gum disease, mouth ulcers, tummy contractions, you name it – but does she complain about them? Hell, no! Bonnie has a sour character. She's like a tough old broad, despite her tiny fragile frame.

Her sweet, kind guardians, Steve and Tracy, who both adore all their cats, always want what is best for Bonnie. I hadn't heard from them for a while but today they contacted me because they wanted to check in with Bonnie and they e-mailed over a couple of questions to see what she was feeling in herself and about the other cats in the family.

Once I'd made contact with Bonnie through her photo, I asked her how she was feeling.

Bonnie may be ancient, but she's a warrior and is quick to say so. 'I'm still fighting. No one's pushing me out yet,' she shouted. Then, just to clarify, 'I hate people feeling sorry for me.'

'How do you feel about Gus?' I asked her.

'Big fat oaf!' she replied.

'How about Chandy, the recent arrival?'

Bonnie answered sardonically, 'Our invader? Well, why not add another one? One more won't make any difference.'

Tracy is a bit of a self-confessed worrier when it comes to her feline family and that definitely includes Bonnie. 'I just worry about her so much,' she said to me. 'I worry whether she is warm enough, whether she's eating enough and whether she's in any pain.'

Bonnie wanted to stop this worry once and for all – it wasn't good for Tracy *or* Steve. So she replied rather harshly, 'Stop whining. Everything's OK. Just get on with it – this is life. We all get old. We all go eventually. I'm not sad.'

What more can you say?!

❧ *The Genteel Hamster* ❧

It makes no difference to an animal whether they are on Earth or in heaven, they continue to care for the sentient beings they leave behind. When animals communicate from the Other Side their communication is as clear as day and often it can be hard to distinguish between animals in spirit and animals in their physical body.

Amy asked for a communication with her hamster, Bunsey, who had passed over. She needed to hear she was OK.

Looking at Bunsey's photos, I could see she had long black hair with a thick white band around her middle, which classified her as a Syrian hamster. She had an attractive white belly, large delicate black ears, a pink tail and perky black whiskers. When I connected with her I could sense her gentle eyes gazing back at me. I sensed her sweet, busy energy and her very inquisitive nature. She showed me she would get Amy's attention by standing up at the edge of her cage when she wanted her to pick her up. She also pictured herself lying on Amy's chest, which she said was her favourite place to fall asleep. She pictured her cage and I could sense how house-proud she was, always keen to show off her home to new friends.

Amy absolutely loved Bunsey and was grieving badly for her. She was worried that she was unhappy in heaven without her.

Bunsey answered Amy's questions and also used the opportunity to give her a piece of advice. She replied, in a voice that was both polite and refined, 'I'm very happy. No pain now, dear.' Her genteel and motherly nature shone through her words: 'Just tell her I love her. And to keep busy. We're all stronger than we appear and we're important too. What we do counts, so keep going, dear. Don't give up so easily – keep going and you'll make me very proud.'

Amy wrote to me about her experience and I feel it would be useful to include it here, especially for the guardians of hamsters and other smaller creatures who are often overlooked:

My love connection with Bunsey was more than I had ever dreamed possible with an animal. I'd had animals in the past, but nothing like Bunsey. Our connection was instant. Hamsters just aren't like that normally. Usually it can take weeks to form a bond and months to get really close.

Her passing devastated me, especially as I had no knowledge of what happened to hamsters' souls after death. The majority of literature I read on the subject only referred to large animals such as cats, dogs and horses. During my research I came across the topic of animal communication and felt that a communication with Bunsey would put my mind at rest and bring some closure to my grief.

Before the reading with Pea, I imagined that hamsters could only use very simple language or just communicate in pictures and feelings. I was surprised by how eloquently Bunsey spoke. Her personality came across accurately during the communication and I had no doubt that it was really her who was speaking. For example, she loved to fall asleep on my chest, which is a very unusual thing for a hamster to do.

Having the communication with Bunsey totally changed how I see hamsters. I now see them as equals and friends rather than in a mother–child or owner–pet relationship. My relationship with Bunsey still affects my life and I hope it always will. I still think of her, especially during hard times, and imagine her support and love. I've had a lot of hamsters since, but none has quite matched my connection with Bunsey. I feel honoured and blessed to have had her touch my life.

❧ *Feathers from Heaven* ❧

If an animal you have loved has passed over, how many times have you wished for a sign that he or she is OK? Many clients consult me because they wish to know their animal companions are safe in heaven. Some people believe white feathers appear as a sign from loved ones who are on the Other Side.

My client Judy, whose story about Lily I related earlier, told me that she'd been asking Lily to give her a sign that in some way she was still with her. She needed to know she was all right and asked her to send her a white feather. On an emotional level Judy wanted to believe in the symbolism of white feathers, but on a rational level she found it hard to trust that feathers weren't just appearing by chance. She put this to the test by saying, 'Lily, I want to see a feather.' And sometimes she did, but most times she didn't. Then she began to be more specific, 'Lily, I want to see a feather in the next 30 minutes.' She ran this test for months and months. This time 90 per cent of the time feathers appeared as requested, but Judy was still not convinced.

Then one day she was out on a country walk in France with her husband. They were walking alongside a field and could see a load of ducks about 200 yards away. They had been talking about Lily and Judy began to cry. She told Steve, 'I really miss her. I can't live without her.' She said again, 'Lily, please send me a white feather.'

Steve joked, 'There's no point asking for a feather now, not with all these ducks here.'

Seconds later, they rounded a corner and were amazed by what they saw. There wasn't *one* white feather, there were *thousands* of them! It was as if a couple of duvets had been ripped open. The tiny feathers reached about 16 feet in one direction and 5 feet in another and were piled on top of each other ankle-deep.

'Oh my God!' they both exclaimed, looking at one another, and then they began to laugh hysterically.

They literally had to kick their way through the feathers to pass, but there were no ducks or people nearby, so how could this be?

About 20 minutes later they returned along the same route with the idea that they would collect a few of the feathers and take them home. If they'd been surprised the first time, this experience would astonish them. Once they reached the spot, there wasn't one white feather to be seen – they'd *all* gone. It was this that convinced Judy that Lily had responded to her plea. She couldn't rationally explain how so many feathers could be there one moment and gone so very shortly after-wards – every single one of them.

❧ *The Goldfish Loves Rock!* ❧

One day I received a call from a lady based in the West Midlands who asked me to communicate with her goldfish, Fred. She didn't have a photo to send me but I was touched when she spoke lovingly of him, so we arranged a telephone appointment to see whether I could communicate without the use of a photo. I asked her to picture Fred and I set my intention to link in with him by using their love connection.

Once I'd made a connection with the goldfish I asked him to describe his tank, what was inside it, in both colour and shape, exactly where it was positioned in the home and also what he could see from his vantage point.

He showed me the tank was based in the sitting room and he could see through into the kitchen. Not only that, the layout of the flat meant anyone coming in or going out had to pass him so he knew, at any given time, where his guardian was and also her boyfriend. He loved being at the hub of things and was adamant he needed to be a central part of the family.

Then he sent me a feeling of loneliness. He pictured another goldfish, who I sensed was female, and I felt a huge amount of love. He continued by picturing himself alone in the tank and then I realized his girlfriend had ascended. He was able to describe her character to a tee. He was also able to tell me his guardian had been away for a number of weeks and she confirmed she'd just come out of hospital.

Furthermore, to totally blow us both away, he shared with us his taste in music. In my mind, I heard the heavy clash of drums and grating electric guitars. 'Rock music?' I said to him. 'You like rock music?'

Again, I heard the sound of drums and guitars.

'Fred likes rock music,' I told his guardian.

'You're kidding!' she said. 'That's my boyfriend's music, his favourite. He plays it in the sitting-room at full blast.'

❧ *'Ti Amo'* ❧

As Fred showed, animals do fall in love. Nowhere was this clearer than when I was teaching my first international workshop in Rome to a room full of animal-loving Italians. In this case the animal with lustful desires was a tortoise called Scopino.

At the end of Saturday afternoon he entered the room as one of the guest teachers. He had been kept waiting all day and I felt his feelings of frustration and annoyance. I'd laid out a comfortable spot for him, but he wasn't interested. Within moments of standing in the centre of our circle he'd decided he was bored and begun to go walkabout. I asked him where he was off to and heard the words, 'To meet everyone.' I received his thoughts in a language I could understand – English – and the Italian students received his messages in their native tongue.

I carried our carapace-shelled land-dwelling reptile around to meet and greet people, one by one. He liked to linger for a moment, his beady eye honing in on the human animal looking back at him. When we reached the seventh person I heard him as loud as an elephant's trumpeting call: 'I *lurrve* her! I *lurrve* her!'

This was Silvia: blonde hair, pretty face, friendly. She exuded kindness and understanding.

'Scopino has the hots for you, Silvia! He says he *lurrves* you! *Ti amo!*' I told her, in front of the rest of the class. She smiled, embarrassed, and the rest of the students burst into giggles.

We carried on round the room and Scopino continued his meet and greet, taking time to give each person a long and slow look.

'Oooff! She stinks!' he shouted out when meeting one woman. 'She stinks!' He wanted to be moved away.

'I'm so sorry, Francesca,' I said. 'He's being a little less than flattering about your perfume. He says you stink.'

My Italian translator relayed the message and laughter erupted round the room. Francesca herself gasped in surprise. It was obvious that what smelled bad to him smelled good to us and vice versa. For this hardback ancient *tartaruga* was himself incredibly pongy, having been walking in his own urine for the past hour.

Scopino and I completed the circle and I gently placed him back down on the floor. I posed a question so everyone could begin to communicate with him.

As they began, Scopino raced back to Silvia – that's 'raced' tortoise style, in slow, measured but determined steps. I brought him back to the front of the room so everyone could get a good look at his face.

'Get a feel of his character. What's his personality like?' I prompted them.

'He's really confident. He's full of himself and very proud. He likes females. He's crazy about them. Can't get enough of them,' said one student.

'He says he's really sexy,' said another.

'He's totally full of himself,' said a third.

I confirmed that Scopino had a very high opinion of himself and his 'pulling' skills. He came across more like an 'Italian stallion' than the toothless, stumpy-legged, claw-footed creature we could see. The other Italian guest teachers hadn't been like this.

Scopino's guardian was unable to attend the workshop, but she'd prepared a question for us, which I put to the class.

'He has a wife back at home who has just laid a number of eggs. Ask him how many eggs he has waiting for him,' I instructed.

His guardian had written the number down and sealed it in an envelope prior to Scopino's arrival. There was only one sentient being in the room who knew the answer ... Scopino himself.

A minute later the students revealed how many eggs Mrs Tartaruga was watching over: 'Seven.' 'Four.' 'Twelve.' 'Three.' 'Twenty.' 'Five.' 'Seven.' 'Eighteen.' 'Seven.' 'Eight.' 'Eight.' 'Twelve.' 'Ten.'

I heard a voice in my head, similar to my own, but slower and with more of a Romeo tone to it. I told everyone that I'd heard 'Nine' and we all waited with bated breath as the envelope was torn open.

'It's nine!' one of the students grinned. 'It's nine.'

Scopino was by now on his third return voyage to Silvia. I gave up; he was making it perfectly clear where he preferred to be. She picked him up and he remained blissful in her arms for the rest of the communication. He was in *lurrve*!

❧ *A Vision of the Future* ❧

I know how lucky and blessed I am to be able to talk to these great animals. My hope is that this book will allow them to have a voice where often their feelings go unheard.

On one level I hope it lifts the veil of this little understood connection and brings you closer to your animals at home, so you approach them with heightened sensitivity and respect.

On another level I hope that more people will want to develop their own ability so they too can share this special connection with animals. That's people like you …

My wish is to share this with as many people as possible. By creating a buzz about this work, I hope that more and more people will be able to understand that intuitive communication is a very natural way of connecting with animals, which, in turn, will give all the animals around us a chance to feel greater understanding and appreciation.

I hope these stories have weaved a way into your heart and you'll feel you want to share them with your friends, your family and your colleagues. Together let us promote the animals' voices and ultimately their message: love.

Afterword

❧ Continual Development ❧

TO BE A GOOD animal communicator, it's essential to have a love of animals but that's not enough in itself. I feel animal communication, like spiritual development, has many layers and you can't progress to the next level unless you do some work on yourself. Over the years I have had to focus not only on my belief system but also on my own patterns and reactions to situations and people. I've also had to let go of negative patterns of behaviour.

This constant questioning and analysis is probably the hardest element for most people. But to work well as an animal communicator you have to be able to let go of negative emotions and to forgive not only others but also yourself. This is how we progress and become clearer, more heartfelt beings. So, every year I go on courses that will further my self-development and support my work as an animal communicator.

I've also been to see professional mediums, like Colin Fry at the Mind, Body and Spirit Festival, and I took a further course at the College of Psychic Studies. I watched Monty Roberts talking about his love of horses at the National Theatre when *War Horse* was playing there and I learned how he felt and related to them in a non-threatening way using their own behaviour to gain their trust.

One year I had the great honour of meeting Linda Tucker of the Global White Lion Protection Trust and attending her White Lion Dream Workshop. I feel particularly drawn to lions in all their guises. It was amazing to be in a room with people so in tune with white lions and passionate about bringing positive change for them and all species. I left feeling I'd experienced something deeply intuitive and uplifting which would affect me on many levels. I think those lessons are still evolving for me.

The theme that has been strongest for me through all my experiences is learning my own truth, the root of who I am, and I've been drawn to courses or people who have indirectly helped me discover my own personal path. Every part of my life informs my animal communication because learning can be found in everything we do. In the same vein, everything I have done leading up to this moment has been useful.

I feel that to be an animal communicator there has to be an understanding of yourself, not only emotionally, but also physically. Personally, I have found the more in touch I am with my own body, the better my communications flow. For me that's through attending yoga classes or visiting the gym. The more stagnant I am on an energetic level, the harder it is to communicate effectively. If I feel exhausted, I find it hard to communicate, and the same goes for when I am upset. If I'm angry, I don't even attempt it.

Sometimes I'll feel particularly drained after a communication, maybe because it was very emotional or tricky, and rather than pushing myself straight into the next one I have learned to take a break. For me that break has to be in nature. I'll ask Morgan if he fancies going out and we'll head off on our favourite walk. This is our special time together. Morgan has taught me to be present. He'll play up if I allow myself to be distracted by my phone or by listening to music. He likes our walks to be a time when we are fully with one another enjoying the gifts of nature. Even if it's raining I still love it. I find being amongst the trees, smelling the fresh rain or feeling the sun on my skin and listening to the sounds of nature very grounding. It's the way I reset myself. It's my mediation. There's no point trying to communicate if you're feeling burnt out. That's the time to stop.

As animal communicators we are like an instrument that needs to be finely tuned and looked after. We are the channels for information to flow. If the pipes are clogged, there's no flow. But please don't get the wrong idea – I'm not totally virtuous. I also like a regular dose of light and fluffy *Neighbours* or a good glass of wine to unwind. Still, I do believe animal communication is not only a job but a lifestyle. And the more you invest in the work and yourself, the easier it will be for you to be in a positive position to support others.

Occasionally I come across students or clients who wish to turn their back on humankind because they feel hurt or betrayed and only want to open their hearts to animals. Animals themselves don't want this. They don't want us to focus on them to the exclusion of humans. They want us to take the time to listen to everybody. They have taught me that they want us to be open-hearted with all sentient beings, because that's when healing happens and balance occurs. My own journey has led me to be much more compassionate towards people than I ever used to be.

As a professional animal communicator, it's not all about hard work, though. I can invest so much into it – emotionally, physically and spiritually – and then the universe gives wonderful gifts of appreciation in return. There is much more laughter in my life now – with animals, with their guardians, with students attending my workshops and just on a general everyday level. There is also much more awareness and honest connection in my life. I can have really heartfelt conversations with people. I also love being around like-minded people and being able to offer a space where people can meet and become friends. Where else can you talk to someone for hours on end about your cat or your dog and find they don't mind? Friendships blossom on animal communication workshops and they have blossomed for me too. I am now proud to call a handful of my long-term clients my close friends. My journey into animal communication has brought me the very thing the soul longs for – intimacy – and I feel so much richer for it.

I would like to encourage all of you to communicate with animals – those who love you, your friends' companions and also the animals you come into contact with on your travels. It will change your life and the animals' lives too.

❧ Final Note ❧

Just before this book went to print two dear cats passed over to spirit.

Right after Jack ascended, his friend Sooty was also diagnosed with cancer. On 6 November 2009 he died peacefully at home curled up in front of his favourite spot, the Aga. In death, he was the same as he was in life – he chose to go his own way, in his own time. He was 15-and-a-half years old.

A day later, Bluesy ascended peacefully under the loving eyes of her guardians, Lynn and Sandra, at the enviable age of 21-and-a-half years old.

Rest in peace, you formidable felines. We are all richer for having known you.

About the Author

PEA HORSLEY believes that everyone is born with the power to communicate with animals. She draws on everything she has learned to teach workshops in animal communication to all levels of ability.

Pea is also available for private consultations, working both in person and distantly, with every species, across any distance.

For more information on workshops and consultations with Pea, visit: www.animalthoughts.com

or e-mail: pea@animalthoughts.com